Get Companies Chasing You

SUSAN BURKE | Job Search Re-Invention

Copyright © 2016 - Susan Burke
All rights reserved

ISBN-13: 978-1537200132
ISBN-10:1537200135

Contents

The Old School Approach	**8**
Summary	12
Get Companies Chasing You – The Premise	**12**
Why you get hired	14
Summary	19
It's A Comfort Zone Type of Thing!	**19**
CV / Resume	21
LinkedIn	21
Networking	22
Website	23
What's Stopping You?	23
Summary	26
The Absolute Foundations Part 1: Your CV/Resume	**27**
CV/Resume Design	30
Summary	33
The Absolute Foundations Part 2: LinkedIn	**33**
How to Create a Winning LinkedIn Profile	36
Summary	42
Break Down the Four Walls of the Company You Work In	**43**
Summary	47

Treat Yourself as a Business	**47**
Summary	51
The Money is in Your Message	**51**
Summary	56
A Job Search Strategy is not a CV/Resume Strategy!	**56**
See yourself as a business	57
Work smarter not harder!	60
Develop the bait!	60
Find a mentor and invest in yourself	63
How to be successful in your job interview	63
Summary	67
You're Hired - Don't Stop Now!	**67**
Final Word	**71**

My Dad, Jimmy, always said: "Keep it simple". You see we have a tendency to over-complicate things and to make a meal out of them, surely there's a way of making things easier?

My job is to help you work out what you need to do, to take away the doubt so that you can stop second guessing yourself and wondering, "Is this good enough?" I can help you to focus on what you NEED to do so that you don't have to learn via trial and error. The trial and error approach is an expensive gamble, particularly if you are looking for those senior positions. You need to work out - what is the cost of not getting it right first time? Are you prepared to lose that great salary and miss out on those amazing opportunities because you took the gamble and lost?

This is where I come in; I can help you to progress from being the amateur job searcher to getting those opportunities coming in, time and time again, from the people who matter to you, as they are the people that can hire you!

I actively practice what I preach, meaning that I can help you whether you are a freelancer; a job searcher or perhaps even someone who is happily employed but is always on the lookout for the next big opportunity. Whoever, you are – this book is for you.

My Dad always said that "You just need to stand for something". Basically, you need to be DIFFERENT, so say goodbye to being that bland old Vanilla and being the carbon copy of everyone else, and say hello to the new and more visible YOU!

So to my Mum and Dad, who taught me all of this... let the message continue. I'm always thinking of you.

As always "Get Noticed, Get Hired"

Sue x

PS. Throughout this book I will provide you with great tools to help re-invent your job search. I would love to personally invite you to my LinkedIn Group, where you will receive hints and tips not just to gain employment but also to manage your career, starting today. To join my LinkedIn group click here.

Ditch the Old School Job Search Strategy and Land That Senior Position!

The Old School Approach

In what seems like eons ago, finding a job was a pretty simple process. A company would advertise a vacancy in a newspaper, and if the job sounded like a fit, you would apply. The CV/Resumes would flood in, and each would be individually scanned for skills and experiences that match the job description. Then after a series of interviews, you would be hired.

Sorry to break it to you but things aren't so simple anymore. But they ARE better. With the rise of the internet, more and more of the job search process is being completed online. In a study by Microsoft, 89% of Recruiters and HR professionals in the United States surveyed, found it appropriate to consider professional online data when assessing a candidate.

A large proportion of our online professional data is held on LinkedIn. As the largest professional social network, LinkedIn has been a huge part of the hiring process. In fact, 89% of all recruiters report having hired someone through LinkedIn[1].

And it works the other way around as well. More and more of us are looking for jobs on the internet and doing a lot of the research about companies before we even get to the interview stages. LinkedIn

---

[1] http://blog.capterra.com/top-15-recruiting-statistics-2014/

users performed over 5.7 billion professionally-oriented searches on the network during 2012.

You can use the internet to find better jobs. You can research companies before working for them and talk to previous employees on LinkedIn. You can find your dream job without having to apply for a heap of jobs you aren't really sure about and wasting your time going to interviews, only to discover the job isn't right for you. And best of all, you can do it all from your own home.

But with this growing online trend in recruitment we have not stepped up to the new challenge, yes we may have a presence on LinkedIn but do we honestly know hand on heart how to use it, other than seeing it as just a pretty CV/Resume online? We're still expecting the good old fashioned CV/Resume to do ALL of the work for us!

Think of it like booking a holiday. Booking a flight on its own isn't enough unless you're going on a spontaneous trip without any strategy in mind. A well-planned trip will involve booking flights and accommodation, exchanging currency and knowing which activities you want to do.

This is why when people say to me; "Take a look at my Resume/CV?"; "What do you think? Will it get me hired?" The answer is probably no if you want those senior level positions. A CV/Resume is NOT enough, so don't just ask me to check it – ask me to CHECK your Job Search Strategy too, and your LinkedIn profile, your interview skills, your branding and all of the other job search tools you have in your toolbox.

Yes, I can work on this and improve it but just like the example above, you need to do more. You need to learn to get companies chasing you, and I will explain how to do this and how to make this your best strategic advantage!

It's no longer good enough to believe that just a quality CV/Resume and good work experience will get you hired or promoted. You need to prove it!

It's more than that. You need to leverage your skills and experience in order to be desired by employers. If you don't? Well, the consequences are that you will struggle to get hired, or your salary will actually decrease. Seriously, it goes down because people can't see the value you can bring!

A number of my clients are coming to me because this is the issue they face. The jobs are below their pay grade, and they now want to get back to the money they were once earning (if not, more!), but they are struggling to show the value they can provide. Are you falling into this trap? Or might you?

If you're reading this, it means you're willing to try something new, which is the first step! And if you don't already know, you should know that the problem isn't with YOU, it's with your strategy and reading this book will help you change that.

Up until now, you will have been applying for jobs ad-hoc with a CV/Resume. You might have a LinkedIn profile that you use, but how strategically are you REALLY using it? How many leads are you following up on? How well do you understand your unique selling point (USP)?

You may have lost some confidence along the way, and that is understandable. Not having a job is frustrating and being in a job you're unhappy with is depressing. We tend to equate our job with self-worth and being unhappy without a job or in a job you hate, can make you feel trapped.

The true cost of NOT being employed is not just monetary.

You can also use this book if you are happy in your job and simply want to get noticed and want to mitigate a disaster such as redundancy. I can show you how to avoid ever being unemployed again by making yourself a highly attractive candidate. In fact why not check out my VIP service "How To Get Companies Chasing YOU[2]"

I have had the great pleasure of speaking to people from all over the world, and I've spoken to some really inspiring people, some of whom have been high-level Directors. The one thing I've learnt is that regardless of your position, level of responsibility or location; people are made redundant - you too could lose your job. I know this is not a great thought, but it's something we need to recognise.

In fact, it may not come down to an involuntary push; you may just decide that you've had enough and want out of your current job. I know from speaking with my clients, that whether by choice or force, it can be really devastating to be out of work.

You see I believe, as I've said before, that we equate our job with self-worth. Being either unemployed or feeling trapped in a job that you can't escape, can spiral us into a cycle of negative thinking and therefore result in a longer span of unemployment. Your talents could be wasted!

As a job seeker, people that are unemployed can find it difficult to deal with the change in routine and those still unhappily employed, can suffer with anxiety from being in a job they absolutely hate (and yes, I've been in the latter situation, but that's another story for another day!)

---

[2] https://www.linkedinsuccessacademy.com/getcompanieschasingyou/

You think getting hired will be pretty easy, but then you realise that it has more or less turned into a daily battle, and that daily battle can be tough!

You update your Resume and LinkedIn profile as advised by all of those websites giving out free tips and yes, that will take you so far, but that's the problem, you're still not hired yet and may not have even been offered an interview.

You don't have a crystal ball, and although you thought it may only take you a couple of months to find some work, now it's stretching further into the abyss!

The daily battle continues but by now, you're actually fighting a daily battle with yourself.

You lose confidence. Hope even.

You feel it will never happen, even if does, can you still do the job?

You question everything.

You still try, though; you still keep applying.

But you feel something is amiss.

You just don't get the results you want, and if you do hit the bullseye, you feel the company is taking the mickey, "Really, you want me to reduce my salary by that much?"

Is this what you have to live with now?

What is the cost to you? It's super easy for me to calculate the financial cost of you NOT getting hired, see *Figure 1* below. However, the real cost is the emotional cost; it's the cost that being on the job market too long can have on you.

Figure 1

The cost of not getting hired!	Loss of earnings UK	Loss of Earnings US	Loss of Earnings United Arab Emirates
Month 2 @ £80,000 (approx. $113,000)	£13,333	$18,833	ﺩ.ﺇ.63,424
Month 2 @ £50,000 (approx. $71,000)	£8,333	$11,833	ﺩ.ﺇ.39,639
Month 2 @ £35,000 (approx. $49,000)	£5,833	$8,166	ﺩ.ﺇ.27,747

It all gets a lot easier when you have someone on your side, someone to help you and something to PUSH you forward when the chips are down! Someone to get you back on track with a strategic plan, not the gung-ho, ad hoc approach you have at present.

Have you had enough of the DIY approach? Is it time to get professional and claim back what you are worth!

Now is the time to remind yourself of everything you have to offer and step up in order to land that next role. Things get easier when you have a little guidance and a push in the right direction.

I have years of experience in careers, and I know that every person is different. This book will give you practical tips and guidance on being hired as a Manager or Executive, that you can personalise to yourself.

Of course, if you want something more tailored, I will also share how you and I can work together[3].

Summary

- 89% of Recruiters and HR professionals in the United States surveyed, found it appropriate to consider professional online data when assessing a candidate.

- 89% of Recruiters report having hired someone through LinkedIn.

- You're not the problem - it's your strategy!

- The true cost of NOT being employed is not just monetary.

- If you continue to use the same methods, expect the same result. It's time to say goodbye to the DIY approach - it's flawed, as you are learning via trial and error. Seriously, what was the salary you're expecting - can you afford to get it wrong?!

Get Companies Chasing You – The Premise

It's not just the internet that has changed, the economy has. We don't keep our positions as long as we used to. It's quite normal to move from one job to the next, looking for better opportunities and more experience.

---

[3] https://sueburkecareers.leadpages.co/consult/

Today, the average time spent in a job is 4.4 years[4]. A huge 91% of millennials don't expect to be in a job for more than three years and along with that, a freelance economy was also born – the world of the Entrepreneur has arisen! As a result, we have to be more creative with how we present ourselves and our CV's/Resumes.

Take my job, for example; a career coach used to visit you at your home or ask you to visit their office. You had to find a service nearby, but now, with advances in technology, you can hire a global career coach anywhere in the world.

A coach like me can work from the comfort of their own home, scheduling meetings face-to-face over the internet. Everything can be planned and calculated with the push of a button - see how far things have changed in such a small space of time and things are still changing!

"Digital is the main reason that just over half of the companies on the Fortune 500 have disappeared since the year 2000," according to Pierre Nanterme, CEO of Accenture.

In the same sense, job seekers can decide to work in any state or any country in the world that they want to. Of course, you already know this, but what I am trying to say to you is that you can't get the job you want by fluke or accident.

You have to make a conscious effort to stand out. If you can harness this amazing power, you will be able to turn the tables on recruitment and have companies chasing YOU.

I get a lot of people asking me to check their CV or Resume. While I'm always happy to do this, I also always stress that you're not going to land this job simply because of what's in your CV/Resume. (definitely for those senior positions!)

Remember I said that you should think of your job like arranging a holiday? It's not just about booking the flight (which is how I see your Resume/CV), there's a whole range of things you need to organise to make sure your trip goes smoothly.

You can think of me very much like a travel agent. I'll help you manage your expectations, overcome challenges, find the destination, weigh up

---

4   http://www.forbes.com/sites/jeannemeister/2012/08/14/job-hopping-is-the-new-normal-for-millennials-three-ways-to-prevent-a-human-resource-nightmare/

your options and see you off.

So let's start with managing your expectations. You have to remember the following;

1. You have failed to recognise there should be more to your approach. Yep, there is a lot more to it, especially when you are gunning for a senior or executive level position.
2. What is your Job Search Strategy? By the way, sending your CV/Resume to every vacancy is NOT the only way!
3. Have you built a two-way funnel? – That is, have you formulated a strategy to get people to recognise YOU?
4. Have you mastered the art of interview – so that when you get in front of the Hiring Manager you have nailed it? Can you improve?
5. Are you failing to recognise you need help? The first step is acceptance! Your CV/Resume is often seriously lacking, but you don't recognise that you're probably suffering from "CV/Resume Shame" check out *page 27* to see if you are falling guilty of this!
6. Stop blaming yourself and using excuses like; "I'm too old" or "I'm too young". The reality is often much simpler than this – you're just not selling yourself.

Why you get hired

So let's start by ingraining this statement into your mind: **a company will only hire you because they have a problem, and they want you to fix it!**

So the new way is recognising this first statement, repeat it to yourself if you need to, this concept is so important…

A company will only hire you because they have a problem and they want you to fix it!

This is why, whatever you produce in terms of your Resume/CV or LinkedIn profile, needs to articulate this.

Think about this for a second and try to grasp what I'm saying. If a company does not have a problem or issue, then they simply don't need staff. It's at times like this that a company will downsize.

So when you're looking to be hired, you have to show your prospective employer that you are the answer to their problems!

This message needs to be articulated in your CV/Resume, your LinkedIn profile and everything else you do to get hired.

Now if you manage to understand this fully, this will stop you from listening to the other 'so called' experts out there.

I work differently to other career coaches. I recognise that you are pretty much perfect the way you are. What I am looking to do is to help you articulate yourself better, where it really matters, which will help you to secure that all-important job.

By helping you to understand exactly what it is that companies are looking for, we have a greater chance of success together. My philosophy is derived from the following three core goals:

1. **You're the Service Provider** - you develop your employer toolkit i.e. your CV/Resume, LinkedIn profile and website (if applicable), with the organisation in mind.

2. **You're the Problem Solver** - you recognise a business only employs staff because they have a problem to solve. If they did not have a problem, they wouldn't need you! You get hired because you can fix those issues.

3. **You're the Communicator** - you recognise the need to communicate your message in a clear, concise way, focusing on your Unique Selling Point (USP) and combining this with what the company needs! Learning to do this can not only help you get hired, but it has numerous other benefits. It can redundant-proof your job and help to build you as a brand so that you never have to apply for a job again.

All of the services I offer are built by living and breathing this concept so if you don't see this as the right strategy for you, basically stop reading now! Additionally, this is what I stand for, this is, in fact, MY Unique Selling Point, this is what makes me different from other career coaches! I actively believe every job seeker, freelancer, employee needs to understand this:

① BREAK DOWN THE 4 WALLS & GET COMPANIES CHASING YOU!

Unless your reputation transcends the four walls where you work; you're always going to be stuck back at square one when you next want to get hired! Break the cycle and build the 'like, know, trust factor' before you even get to that stage!

② TREAT YOURSELF AS A BUSINESS

Recognise that you only get hired for one reason ►► You solve an employer's problem. Treat yourself as a business and create your Resume/CV and LinkedIn profile with this in mind!

③ THE MONEY IS IN YOUR MESSAGE!

End the vanilla status and stop the carbon copy. It's time to become real and stop that nonsensical paraphrasing on your longwinded CV/Resume. Say goodbye to boring buzz words, writing that you are "a forward-thinking, hands-on, think out of the box employee" won't get you anywhere. Let's stop sending the Hiring Manager to sleep!

④ CREATE A JOB SEARCH STRATEGY & BIN THE AD HOC APPROACH

Wouldn't it be nice if you knew exactly what you needed to do every single day in order to get hired and build a 2-way funnel where interested companies are seeking you out? Well, you can. Learning via trial and error won't help – you need to do this properly.

No job is for life these days, so how are you protecting yourself from redundancy? Branding and positioning yourself is key!

With a new Job Search Strategy, you will be able to build contacts and connections in your industry so that prospective employers already know you. This is basically how you mitigate the most negative possible outcomes.

Changing your approach to job search is how you will get opportunities coming to you.

If the rest of the population is doing it a certain way…that in itself is enough of a reason to change your approach. You're just blending in you see? You can learn how to step out and be seen. I promise you one thing, unless you're prepared to STEP forward and be noticed, how do you ever expect to get hired?

My catch phrase is: "Get noticed, Get hired". Companies don't read boring CVs/Resumes and unattractive LinkedIn profiles because they don't emphasise what you can do for them!

I see people all the time getting so stressed out about things they don't have control over. STOP, it's stress that is totally avoidable!

So let's focus less on things we can't control and more on the things we can.

Sounds simple and trust me, I'm guilty of falling into the trap just as much as the next person. That low feeling and difficulty in selling yourself. That feeling you will never find something, or wanting to give up, but these negative thoughts will never benefit you.

So I would love to create a movement to make Job Search fun, to actually embrace it. The only way you can do this is to go with the things that you actually have control over.

If you start to worry over the things you can't control, you get scared, and when this happens, we tend to stick our heads in the sand and do absolutely nothing! Zero, zilch!

We've all worked for companies where you can see the writing on the wall. The business is struggling, and people are scared and are clinging on for dear life, hoping it won't be them that is sacrificed. The thing is, when this happens, this is your chance to rise up and it could actually be the making of you – embrace the challenge, don't run from it.

When you take ownership of it and say it out loud, those sleepless nights no longer have that power over you - because YOU'VE taken control. That's the secret! That's the type of movement I want to create, one that empowers everyone to take action, no matter how small, each and every day.

One that allows you to take back ownership for YOU. DITCH THE STUFF YOU CAN'T CONTROL AND GO WITH THE THINGS YOU CAN... and if you want to beat yourself up, don't bother - it's a waste of emotion, this won't help you.

Go with what you can actually control.

What you can't control	What you can control
Getting hired next week at interview.	1. Practice your mock interview skills before the big day. Ask a friend to assist, or seriously up your game and use someone like me, the service I offer is called "Be the One at Interview" [https://www.linkedinsuccessacademy.com/interview-101-get-you-hired/].
	2. I personally believe every job seeker should have this in their job search toolkit, as you will utilise this so many times over the course of your career, it's called the "Interview Toolkit" [https://www.linkedinsuccessacademy.com/interview-toolkit-4/] and it comes with a blue print for how to present yourself at interview.
	3. You can start creating a name or brand for yourself well before the interview to put you at a competitive advantage. Imagine the Hiring Manager knowing who you are – before you even walk into that office! Check out my 20-minute podcast [https://www.linkedin.com/pulse/20-minute-training-get-you-hired-free-from-bootcamp-job-susan-burke?trk=prof-post] to help you achieve just that! That's also your competitive advantage – if seven other people are also being interviewed and the recruiter has heard of you, well it's not rocket science – that can only be a positive.
Getting made redundant.	Sometimes we have a feeling this could happen, call it your "gut feeling" and listen to it! Start considering your Plan B. Whilst you're still employed you could hire a career coach to get you ready. You could start setting up a LinkedIn profile and CV/Resume, as well as getting training in order to develop new skills.
Getting stressed out and worrying about money or life because you don't have a job.	Get that professional help sooner rather than later, have a plan of how to effectively spend your time. Focus on what you need to do each day to get hired, you may have to consider a job hopping strategy (get yourself any job) just to get some cash flowing through the door!

The new approach is about getting noticed. In very basic terms, it's about being: LIKED, KNOWN and TRUSTED. This is the LKT Factor and to achieve this, you have to ask yourself, 'What makes you different?' The new approach to job search I am talking about is, where you can be YOU. A note to oneself, you see you don't need to be better, you just need to be different.

Summary

- A job isn't for life anymore. You need to protect yourself from redundancy.
- Admit that the way you have been doing it, doesn't work anymore. If you want to get hired, you have to start by changing your approach.
- Start by managing your expectations and realising what is within your control and what isn't. Focus more on what you can control and forget the rest!
- Create a Job Search Strategy that builds a two-way funnel so companies recognise YOU.

It's A Comfort Zone Type of Thing!

I can say that I love my job – can you?

I've worked with some amazing people from all around the world, and I've shown them how to get past the 'I don't know how to sell myself' barrier. In fact, we have smashed it down!

The only thing you need to know to get hired is how to sell yourself. It might not happen overnight, but it's a really simple formula.

Start by harnessing the power of your unique selling point (USP). Remember that every employer has a problem that they want you to solve, and you can show them how you can do that with your USP.

So yes, I do practice what I preach, if you missed it, please see below and there is more about my own USP on *page 15*. What's yours?

① BREAK DOWN THE 4 WALLS & GET COMPANIES CHASING YOU!

② TREAT YOURSELF AS A BUSINESS

③ THE MONEY IS IN YOUR MESSAGE!

④ CREATE A JOB SEARCH STRATEGY & BIN THE AD HOC APPROACH

Working out your USP and developing your message isn't easy, I'm not going to lie to you, and this message will evolve over time, in the roles you do, in the person you become because we are always learning – aren't we? Mine sure has!

This is where my skill lies; I can help you to work out what your message is by assisting you and helping you to see what you stand for and most importantly why this matters to the company who should hire you!

Let's take a look back through your tools:

- CV/Resume
- LinkedIn
- Website (If applicable to you. The people that I feel a personal website is key for, are those in the Creative Sector, you need to SHOW what you do – think portfolio!)
- Networking
- Branding

Are you really utilising these to your full potential? Have you thought about your USP yet?

Your USP is all about the WHY. Why are you doing this? Why should an employer hire you?

Take a minute now and really think about this. Write some ideas down on a piece of paper. This is the foundation of you as a brand. These are the bricks that you want to build your entire hiring strategy on.

We'll go through some of these in more detail later in this book, but for now, let's have a look at the key items:

CV / Resume

The first thing you need to do is update your CV/Resume. Employers receive stacks of CVs/Resumes in their hands every day. What are you going to do to stand out? This is why I actually created my Resume/CV Store because I was sick and tired of the bland CVs/Resumes[5] out there!

Designing your CV/Resume is a no brainer. With a little bit of thought, you can make something plain, stand out and grab the attention of a prospective employer.

Now that you've got someone to read your CV/Resume, what are you going to say about yourself? How are you going to show a prospective employer that YOU are the solution to their problem?

Well, I hope it's not by using a bunch of phoney adjectives such as; determined, hard-working, punctual, creative, team worker, etc. – *blergh*!

An employer doesn't want to hear a bunch of fancy adjectives. They want to hear what you've done. They want your story. So tell them.

Use stats and figures to back yourself up. What did you do for the last company you worked for? How does it relate to the problem you are going to solve for this company?

This takes some clear thinking in order to articulate the message you want to relay and some active promotion in order to drive it home to your niche/field/industry; your community and the people who are interested in what you've got to say.

Lastly make sure you create a second version of your CV/Resume, which is only going to be read by the recruitment agencies. You can download a robot friendly CV template here[6].

LinkedIn

Your LinkedIn profile is like a mini online portfolio. A place where you can showcase your professional profile and network online. It's a lot more than just an online CV/Resume.

Your USP is just as important on LinkedIn. You only have a short space of time from when someone looks at your profile to make yourself stand out and to do so you need to remember why a company

---

5   *https://www.linkedinsuccessacademy.com/cv-store/*
6   *https://sueburkecareers.leadpages.co/executive-cv-resume-template-bundle/*

should hire you over anyone else.

LinkedIn is indexed in Google's search engine results pages. So Google will scour your LinkedIn pages for keywords and present your profile to people looking for the same things. If you can find the right keywords for your USP, you can optimise your profile to be found under these terms.

LinkedIn also has a publishing tool where you can publish blog posts and increase your potential of being found this way.

If you haven't yet got a LinkedIn profile, set one up NOW!

There are 433 million people on LinkedIn[7] from all around the world. This tool is the easiest way to reach a wider audience fast.

If you do have a LinkedIn profile, look at how many recommendations you have. Could you have more?

Well, don't be scared! Get up and ask your clients and colleagues to recommend you! This is your career we're talking about. If you think you have done something positive, ask someone to recommend you. After all, you would do the same for someone else, right?

Use the template for asking for recommendations that I'm giving away on *pages 41 and 42*.

Networking

Today, you can network both online and offline, but a good mixture of both is key to your success.

LinkedIn has Groups and search features which will help you target potential prospects and start conversations with people in order to build relationships…

Relationships that turn into business opportunities.

Again you need to take yourself out of your comfort zone. Online is very much the same as face-to-face networking. Think of it like being at a party of neurosurgeons and talking about car engines; you're not going to get very far. Your key is to fit your 'WHY YOU' into the interests and goals of the employer.

You don't go to a dinner party and spend the whole night talking about yourself either. You start a conversation about the other party's deeper

---

[7] http://www.statista.com/statistics/274050/quarterly-numbers-of-linkedin-members/

interests and build a relationship that way. Well, this is EXACTLY what you need to be doing in LinkedIn Groups and at networking events.

Stop procrastinating. Just do it!

Website

It costs next to nothing to get yourself a domain name and build a website, portfolio or even a blog and with today's new tools and technologies, you don't even need to hire a website designer. You can build your own website on WordPress or Wix with just a few clicks of a button. Wix is great because it's FREE!

So what's stopping you?

You need to have an online presence so that you can direct people from your CV/Resume and LinkedIn profile to your website or blog. This is where people can find out more about you and how you can help them.

If you're in the creative industry, build an online portfolio to showcase your work. If you're a business service, build a blog to add value and share your experiences and successes. If you work in a highly technical field, build an online community for your niche through a forum or blog.

What's Stopping You?

All of this takes time, but you have to be dedicated if you want to attract a prospective employer. If you're unemployed now, you could be spending the working day doing this! You don't even have to get out of your jogging bottoms; it just means you have to get your brain moving. Start strategising about getting that job!

Have you got great intentions but those intentions never seem to see the light of day?

Or maybe you have begun but it's not a cohesive plan, you keep stopping and starting with no end goal, and let's face it, it's starting to get you down.

You're not alone. However, you do need to make a decision as to what you want. Remember that by not doing anything; you are unconsciously deciding to stay where you are.

The only thing in life that you have no real choice over is taxes and death (not very motivating), however, what is motivating, is that you and only YOU are in control of what you do or don't do each day and where you end up.

So how do you overcome procrastination, well firstly, you need to define it. According to Wikipedia...

> *"Procrastination is the practice of carrying out less urgent tasks in preference to more urgent ones, or doing more pleasurable things in place of less pleasurable ones, and thus putting off impending tasks to a later time, sometimes to the "last minute" before a deadline."*

If you understand this, it's only the first part in beating it. It's kind of like dieting; you can read every book on how to diet or read about celebrities dieting dilemmas, but this won't actually help you to lose weight! YOU have to DO the real work, which is exercise and eating more healthily. The art of reading book after book won't get you far...you will still be overweight!

YOU just need to CHOOSE.

This is why I want you to consider after you've read this book – what's next for you?

1. Want to see the value I can offer, in a low cost, risk free way, then I promise you - you will love the "Career Unplugged Society Membership Programme[8]" designed to get companies chasing you. Learn how to get that job and how to actively manage your career.

   This membership programme is great for job seekers and those in their current job who recognize the old approach basically sucks – learn how manage your career & take back control now – this is like riding a bike once you know, you will have this skill for life!

2. Prefer some individual VIP attention? This is great for people who are in their jobs or want to get there next opportunity. Check out the "Get Companies Chasing YOU – The actual Blueprint[9]" Want to schedule a complimentary session to see if this right for you?[10]

3. I'm here to support you all the way with my VIP range, book in for a Breakthrough Job Search Session now to learn the No 1 why you're not getting the job you want[11]. I do my best to accom-

---

8 https://careerunplugged.com

9 https://www.linkedinsuccessacademy.com/getcompanieschasingyou/

10 https://susanburkecareers.acuityscheduling.com/schedule.php?appointmentType=1696046

11 https://susanburkecareers.acuityscheduling.com/schedule.php?appointmentType=1160277

modate everyone who applies for these sessions, but my time is limited each week I don't ever turn anyone away and regardless of whether I can offer you all of my personal attention or not, I will at least be able to point you in the right direction as to how you should move forward. Therefore, this is a win/win situation for you!

So let's make this simple for you. You need to choose to move forward and not to stay still, and you need to do this by taking action. Don't worry it doesn't need to be a massive amount of action, but it does need to be consistent. I understand you have a life, and you may already have a job, but small consistent changes can and do make huge differences.

Here are some examples of what you could do:

- Refresh your CV/Resume
- Update your LinkedIn profile
- Ask and gain recommendations from people within your industry
- Network online in groups
- Attend that networking meeting

You kill procrastination, by being aware that you're suffering with it and by taking some action, no matter how small.

You kill procrastination by realising that you can control it.

You kill procrastination with consistent action.

You can do anything you set your mind to.

- If you wanted to write a book and this is on your bucket list – well you can!
- If you want to be known in your field and increase your salary – well you can!
- If you want a new job – you can!
- If you want job opportunities to come to you – well make it happen, build your two-way funnel to get people interested in you and what you can offer!

Procrastination can be beaten with a simple formula:

1. Scheduling the time in a calendar.

2. Being more organised.
3. Being consistent.
4. Being motivated

If you are serious about getting hired and are ready to take action NOW, then I would like to invite you to request a 60-minute breakthrough session with me, in which I will clearly show you why YOU are not getting hired or how to position yourself, so that you can reduce the cost of learning via trial and error! Please note there is a limit to the complimentary consultations I can provide however, I don't turn anyone away. I will be able to point you in the right direction as to how to move forward, meaning it is a win/win situation for you!

> **WHAT YOU SHOULD EXPECT IN A BREAKTHROUGH SESSION.**
>
> - Learn to create a sense of clarity in your job search about how to get the job you really want to have.
>
> - Discover the essential building blocks you need to make this happen.
>
> - Determine the number one thing stopping you from getting the job you want.
>
> You can book here[12]

Summary

- You've been in your comfort zone for too long. It's time to step outside and try something new!

- Start by realising your unique selling point and make sure this encompasses everything you do.

- Build strong foundations with your CV/Resume and LinkedIn profile.

- Expand to a personal website and then start networking to build relationships.

- Stop procrastinating. Start scheduling time in your calendar and be consistent.

---

[12] https://susanburkecareers.acuityscheduling.com/schedule.php?appointmentType=1160277

The Absolute Foundations Part 1: Your CV/Resume

A house never stays standing when it's built on weak foundations, and like a house, the strength of your foundations will determine how strong and withstanding your Job Search Strategy will be.

In your job search, your foundations are your CV/Resume and your LinkedIn profile.

I get so many CVs and Resumes pass through my door that are well, BLAND. Maybe it's because we're conditioned to think ours need to follow the same formula as everyone else's. This is what I call, suffering from "CV/Resume Shame".

Not everybody likes my honesty, but wouldn't you prefer that I just told you the simple truth rather than let you carry on using that CV/Resume when you're never going to get the results you want from it? Check out my video "What I hate about CV/Resume Writing companies[13]."

Please don't shoot the messenger, but most of you just sound like a thesaurus. Yes, you've managed to squeeze some juicy adjectives into your CV/Resume and probably as many as you can into one paragraph – am I right? I know I'm harsh, but it just doesn't work using big words unless you can back them up with evidence and statistics!

Go and check your CV/Resume this second, have you done this?

No proof right? No statements to back up that you've actually got these skills? No evidence to show where and how you have put them into practice and what difference they have made to the company? I didn't think so.

If you can't evidence what you've written – you're just blowing random words into the wind, and it's just a waste of time and space.

Take a look at the CV/Resume in the box below; it sounds good but it's all just filled with fluffy adjectives, and when you look deeper you realise there is no meaning. It will get lost amongst a heavy pile of CV/Resumes all doing the same thing.

---

13 https://youtu.be/3ID7QkO90Vk

> John Smith
>
> Accountant
>
> **Summary Profile**
>
> I've worked in finance for over 15 years. During this time, I have personally shown to excel as a strategic and forward thinker for the company. I have undergone numerous projects which, with my input have been very successful. This is due to my ability to manage teams and always bring a positive attitude to any challenge.

BORING! This guy is doing exactly what EVERYONE ELSE IS DOING!

It's average at best!

Ask a Hiring Manager whether can they spot a decent Resume/CV – of course they can. They can spot it a mile away.

If you go through a recruitment company, there's a good chance that your CV/Resume won't ever make it to a company because the recruitment company will spot your vanilla CV/Resume a mile off – you just sound like everyone else, and they will filter you out!

You don't need a thesaurus – what you need is a way to improve your Resume/CV and this is exactly how I can help you. My VIP package is perfect if you are too busy to dedicate the time to do this yourself. The reason why everyone loves this service is because I provide two Resumes/CVs! I make the 'WHY' a focal part of your Resume in my Infinite Figure Resume Service[14]. I'm pretty old-fashioned in the way I work, regardless of where you live in the world, if I'm going to complete your CV/Resume for you; you and I would need to speak (via Skype for example) so that we can work out your USP.

You're not a graduate anymore. You're an experienced professional looking for an executive position. Where a graduate would spend time highlighting their qualifications, you need to highlight your skills and experience.

A CV/Resume has two kinds of information about you in it. Factual and subjective. Factual information is your name, contact details, address,

---

14 https://www.linkedinsuccessacademy.com/infinite-figure-resume-service/

etc., while subjective information is your personal statement. Generally, it's the subjective information that people find hardest to present.

The trick to getting your CV/Resume spot on is making sure you include the most important piece of information. **Why should this company hire you?**

So create a CV/Resume based on this and you will find a job you will love. You should be going through the job description and specifications of the job you want to be hired for and making sure you include the right information about yourself.

Here is an outline of the types of information you need to include:

Personal profile/statement

This is a key part of the CV/Resume, but don't fill it with vacuous, empty statements that could be about anybody. Your CV/Resume should show who you are, tell the company what you've done, and demonstrate how you are what they want and need. Back your profile up with facts – if a claim cannot be backed up, it's not worth having in there.

Work history

Keep it clear, concise, list your duties and then follow them up with key achievements for every single position you have held. If you can quantify and bullet point your achievements to make them digestible, then that is even better!

Don't cram

Too much information is over the top and who wants to read a novel when they're just looking for a new member of staff? Entice the reader, make them want to go on and think 'wow, I want to see more of this person.' Avoid boring them to sleep until they start yawning or reaching for the coffee, or vodka if it was me!

Testimonials

Often something that is overlooked, but definitely something that I like to include. This isn't as hard to obtain as you might think.

Have LinkedIn? Great! Copy a recommendation that you have from there and paste it into your CV/Resume. If you don't have LinkedIn, then start by asking a few people who you have worked for and see what you can compile.

Your CV/Resume testimonial should rave about you and come from somebody in a higher position.

Associations

Do you belong to any professional associations? If you do, include them, as long as they are relevant to the position you are seeking; they show that you are serious about what you do!

Awards

Won any? If so, sing about them! Before we go on, I mean relevant to your job, not the pub quiz trophy that you got about seven years ago as a fluke! If they are impressive, include them and make sure that you rejig the structure of your CV/Resume to show them off as best as possible. I once worked with a client who had recently won a national Accountancy Award, so I prioritised this to the top of his CV/Resume. Common sense!

Contact details

Make sure that your email address is appropriate. Your CV/Resume should divert me clearly to where I can contact you. If you're on LinkedIn, make sure that it is up to date, a good profile should score highly on Google so even if you don't include it as part of your CV/Resume, the recruiter is still going to find you when they search for your profile online. You can't hide from them! This is why it can't be average!

Call to action

A CV/Resume is only a brief overview of your professional profile. There is so much more a Hiring Manager will want to know about you after they have read it, and they will often go online to find this information out. Give them somewhere they can go from your CV/Resume to see examples of your work, your experience or your expertise. This will be a link to your LinkedIn page, a website or blog.

CV/Resume Design

When a Hiring Manager receives a stack of applications, the best way to stand out from that pile of CV/Resumes is through design. You want your CV/Resume to be eye catching enough to get that Hiring Manager reading yours first. This is your creative CV/Resume template and is sometimes in the form of a PDF or Word template, check out the CV Store[15] for ideas.

You will also need something that will stand out to the Applicant Tracking System (ATS). ATSs are used in most recruitment companies to handle CV/Resumes, job applications, and postings. This computerised system will scour your CV/Resume for keywords, so when a recruitment company has a job posting, they can quickly find all applicants who have the right skills and experience to match the job.

So your second CV/Resume needs to be a computer friendly version filled with keywords, ready for a computer to find you instantly when the right job appears.

Want to actually see a CV/Resume with a solid framework for you to follow, step by step? You can download this CV/Resume here[16].

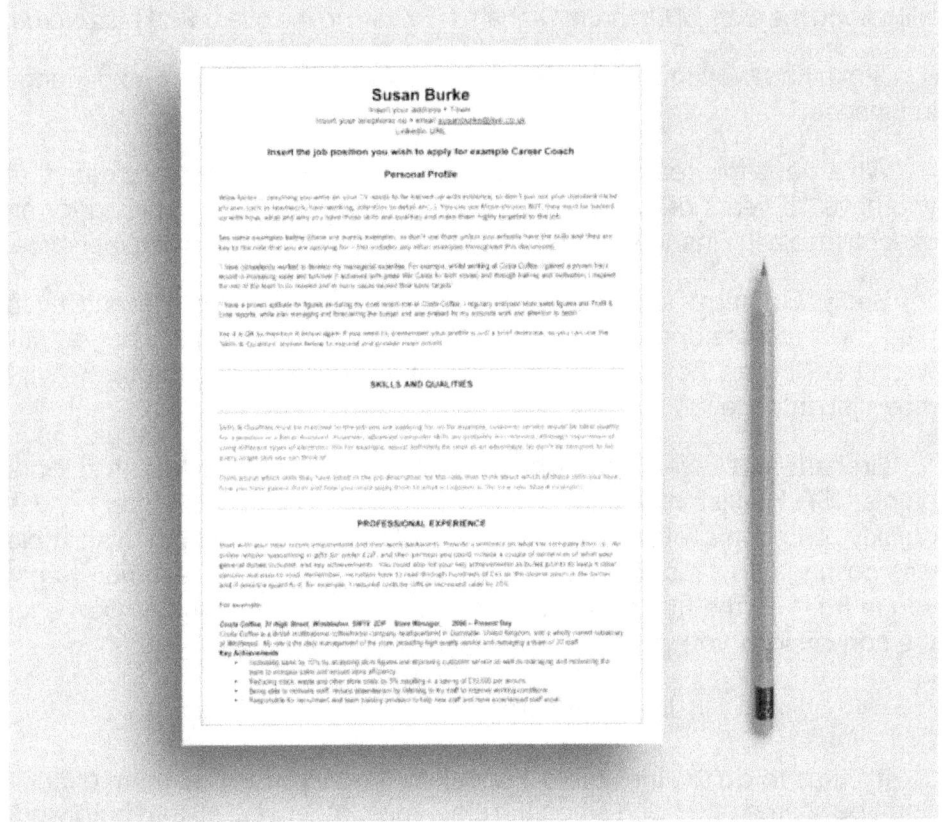

---

15   https://www.linkedinsuccessacademy.com/cv-store/
16   https://sueburkecareers.leadpages.co/executive-cv/

Remember when creating your CV, to stay focused! Don't stray away from anything that doesn't show what you can do for them. You want to hook them in – so make sure you're an attractive bait!

Don't be scared to rejig – you can move things around for each individual job that you apply for. Think what you'd want to read if you were the recruiter, and turn your CV into that.

To make things even easier for you, I created the Infinite Figure Resume Service[17] to help you understand how to create a CV/Resume which is bang on target. No more fluff, no more second guessing yourself.

With any service I offer, we work on your USP in order to answer that killer question: "why should a company hire you?"

To give you an example of the power of the Infinite Figure Resume Service, I will tell you the story of Graham. Graham fell victim to the overuse of buzzwords.

"I'm a hardworking, motivated individual who has 15 years' experience in Finance."

What does this really mean and does a Hiring Manager really care that you have 15 years of experience? It's likely that everyone applying for an executive role in Finance will have the same, if not more years of experience.

Sadly, Graham's entire CV/Resume sounded like this. He had even paid for a professional CV/Resume service to get some help, but he still wasn't seeing an increase in conversions. By conversions (by the way), I mean job interviews!

Graham and I went through his CV/Resume and tweaked it to work on his USP. He instantly started to get more interviews. Soon after he was quickly placed in a job that was £80K or $120,000. Something this simple was costing him a job! Because that's the purpose of CV/Resume - to get you in front on the hiring manger. So if it's not up to scratch, it won't get the conversions you want!

Now you have the perfect CV, what should you do?

It's time to do the inevitable – speak to the recruiter. Call them direct – don't be scared and don't sit on the side-lines, otherwise all that hard work has gone to waste!

---

17   https://linkedinsuccessacademy.com/infinite-figure-resume-service/

Forget about sending an email with an attachment that leaves you hoping for the best, and make sure that you have had a good look through to ensure that nothing needs amending or tweaking to suit the recruiter that you are approaching.

The framework that I have provided you with will get you closer than you've ever been before, so build upon it with your own skills and experience.

Start to develop mutually beneficial relationships and be forthright when it comes to introducing yourself; connect on LinkedIn, pick up the phone – push yourself right to the forefront of their minds so that when the perfect job comes up, you're the first person that springs to mind!

Summary

- Write two CV/Resumes, one for the Hiring Managers and one for the recruitment company's ATSs.
- Make it pop with design.
- Show a company why they should hire you with hard facts.
- Leave out those dreadful adjectives!
- Go further and call the companies you are applying to work for.

The Absolute Foundations Part 2: LinkedIn

There is nothing worse for an employer than having a look for potential candidates on LinkedIn, only to find that they are drowning in a sea of 'motivated self-starters,' who aren't actually even motivated enough to make their profile different from their competitor's.

Employers should look at your profile and scramble to get in touch with you, not sit there scratching their heads wondering what jargon nonsense they just read.

If you sound like a carbon copy of somebody else – you won't get the job, and you won't get results – it's that simple.

It's time to get noticed and get hired!

If you think that once you've tweaked your LinkedIn profile, you will suddenly start getting found as if by magic – then I will just say that there is no such thing as a free lunch.

You see, you've got to have a great profile first (this is the bait – a bit like fishing) but you also need to utilise the huge database that IS LinkedIn.

In order to take advantage of all that LinkedIn has to offer you need to make the most of the company and recruitment searches as well as your existing and potential connections.

All of this personalised and bespoke coaching on how to get the most out of LinkedIn comes as standard. If you wish me to sort out your LinkedIn profile once and for all, the VIP service is called Attract Infinite Job Offers with the LinkedIn Rehab Clinic[18].

However, I don't stop there! I will also provide you with step-by-step directions through The LinkedIn Success Academy[19] so that you always know exactly what you need to do!

Your career is your own personal business, just like mine. When are you going to take ownership for it and make things happen?

If you're not willing to invest in you and your future, why should someone else?

Feel free to check out my four FREE Video Series[20]. It will be a real eye opener in how you can start leveraging your profile 24/7. Here's what **Luis Colasnate, Group Energy Manager** and Head of Economic Research had to say about it:

> "The e-learning proposed by Susan prepared me to use LinkedIn efficiently. Susan has a 360° view and will give you LinkedIn profile tips; ideas on how to use LinkedIn for professional networking and explain how to use LinkedIn for marketing and business purposes. Susan made it easier and what most people don't realise is, if you utilise your LinkedIn profile, you won't even have to look for opportunities."

Take my friend, Jayne Thompson. She left teaching after 25 years, 15 of which were spent in a private girls' school, where she was the Director of Music.

At 50, she found herself unemployed and looking for a change in career. She would never have gone on LinkedIn had she remained in teaching (by the way, teachers you should be on there!). I helped her write her profile and set her on her way. Six months later, she said:

---

18 https://www.linkedinsuccessacademy.com/linkedin-rehab-clinic/

19 https://www.linkedinsuccessacademy.com/linkedin-success-academy/

20 https://sueburkecareers.leadpages.net/linkedin-free-video-training/

> "I started sending connection requests to people in the music industry. Then I broadened this to people in media and the arts. I watched what people wrote in the 'news feed' section like the kind of pictures they used, and I took note of the messages people sent to me. I began sending thank you messages to anyone who connected with me. I always replied to anyone who messaged me. I liked a post and was so pleased when I was publically thanked by the person who had shared the post. I am constantly amazed and pleased at the lovely thoughts and wishes that people have towards each other on LinkedIn, from all over the world. I seem to have quite a following, but at the same time, **I have helped many other people advertise their work**. My advice to anyone on LinkedIn is: be nice, wish people the best, thank people if they do something for you, offer to help people. Since going on LinkedIn; I have become a composer, a manager, recorded my first CD of piano compositions in Spain, and am now working on my second CD. I have met many amazing people, and some rather strange (don't worry, you can always block any weirdos – this is the internet after all). I am happy. The best thing I ever did was leave teaching. If I hadn't, I wouldn't be doing what I'm doing now. I've never been so happy, and LinkedIn has played a huge part in that. Whatever happens, it's important to stay positive. Wishing people well on LinkedIn and receiving well wishes back from all over the world can help you to do this. Having taught composition for 25 years, though never having had a single lesson on it myself, I never thought I'd actually become a composer myself. I began by arranging pieces for my choir, simply because the choice of repertoire and arrangements out there never really impressed me that much. I soon realised that people liked my arrangements, and I began to wonder... Someone told me I should start writing piano music. Had I not lost my job, I would never have started. I write pieces that I would have loved to play when I was younger. Relaxing piano music. I have my CD on in the car and it keeps me calm when the traffic is bad. I tested my first piece by sending blips to some chosen friends on LinkedIn. The response was very good, so I began writing seriously. I posted short sound bites on LinkedIn, and the response was immediate and wonderful".

http://jaynethompson.net

Opportunities will come knocking!

One of the biggest job search crimes out there is the crime of having a terrible LinkedIn profile, and I guarantee that you are committing it.

How can I guarantee it?

Because you're here.

You already know that your LinkedIn profile isn't up to scratch, and you already know that it should be better. So let's sort it.

I'm here to stop you being a part of the epidemic of bad LinkedIn profiles!

How to Create a Winning LinkedIn Profile

Time and time again I see glaring mistakes on LinkedIn profiles. I want to make sure you aren't making any of these mistakes and if you are, well at least you will know, and you can do something about it – fast!

The tips in this chapter will help you revamp your profile into something that will attract Hiring Managers and Recruiters from the first five seconds they look at it.

Headline

Your headline is the first thing people read when they are looking for you on LinkedIn. So what do you want this short chunk of text to say about you? How do you sum up your professional career in just 30-40 characters?

You want your headline to include keywords but still stand out from the crowd, and get a passer-by to click through and read more into your profile.

Avoid terms like 'ninja', 'expert' or 'guru'; these are generic and everyone these days are using these words to describe their abilities. I mean who is really an expert at anything? And if you are an expert would you really call yourself that?

LinkedIn URL

LinkedIn allows you to customise your URL. You should do this so you can include a link on your business card and make it easy for people to look you up. I would say to make it your name if you can! Obviously, if your name is John Smith, this may not be possible!

Summary

Needs to be punchy and grab the hiring manager's attention straight away without using an overdose of fancy adjectives.

Education

Of course by now, you have long since left University/College. This stage is now less likely to affect whether or not you are going to be hired.

If you went to University/College you will want to say **where** and **when** but also tell people which subject(s) you did and what grade you achieved at the end. It's also helpful for people to know if you did a Masters or a PhD.

If you have any other relevant qualifications, you can add them here as well.

Profile picture

I am talking about the picture you use for your profile here, and yes I am also talking to you - if you have no picture! Studies have shown that you are 11 times less likely to be viewed without a picture. There should be no such thing as keeping a low profile on LinkedIn even though I have noticed for some of you; this is how you like it!

They say a picture is worth a 1,000 words and I will prove this to you with the shots below! (*Figure 2*). The selfie picture and the incomplete profile will do absolutely nothing for you. Zero, Zilch!

Figure 2

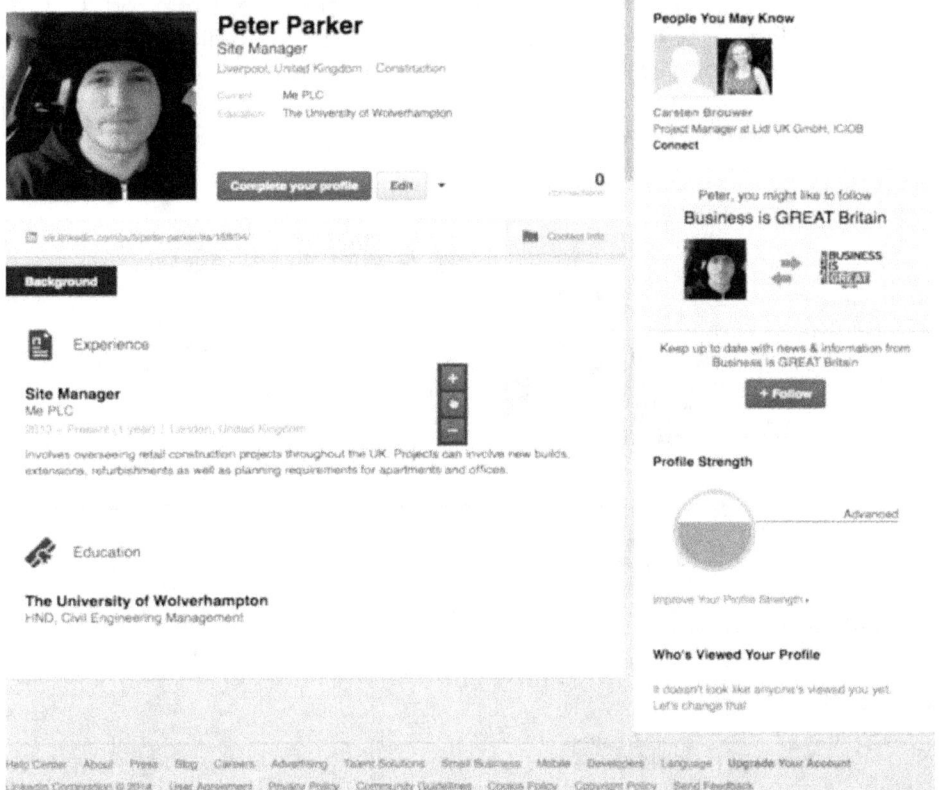

Here are my tips:

- Don't use an avatar picture; I want to see you not a picture of a cute puppy or a cartoon character!

- Do choose a plain background; I don't want to be distracted by your wallpaper or your kitchen in the background.

- Don't have people guessing which one is you in the picture!

- If you have managed to get a pic with a celebrity or your favourite MP, well keep it under your pillow, you don't need it as a LinkedIn profile pic!

- Don't use a 'make do' picture where you have obviously chopped the other person out of the photo.

- Please, no selfies or shots of you on a glamorous night out – these are not appropriate.

- Guys just because you've hit 40 or 50 and you've completed your first marathon, or you've learnt to surf or just got married, I don't need to know this. This is for Facebook, not LinkedIn (unless you're a professional marathon runner or surfer of course).

- So what makes a good picture?

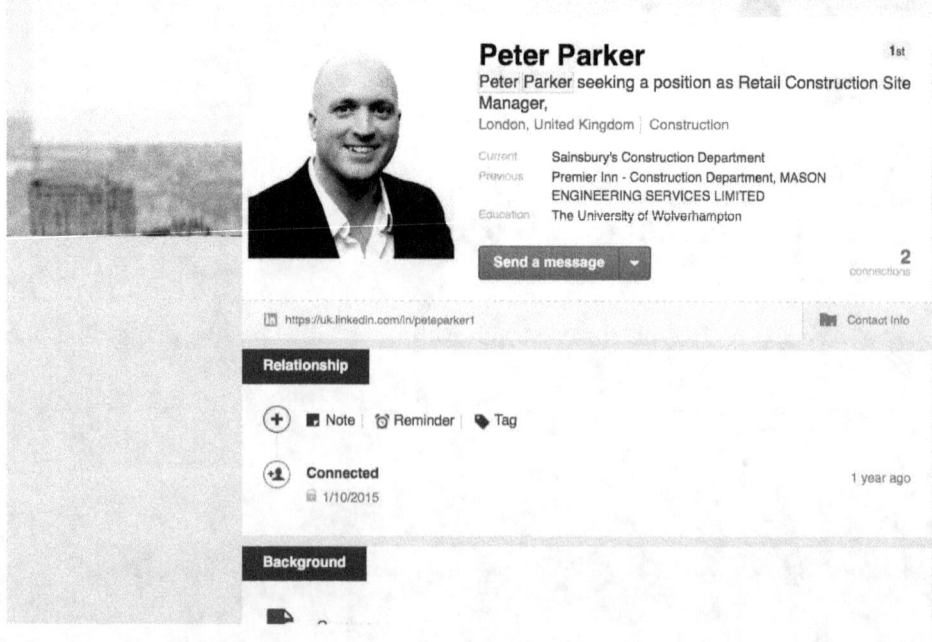

A good picture is a head and shoulders shot of you, ideally without sunglasses or a hat on and without a distracting background.

So, if a picture is worth a 1,000 words, be honest with yourself. What does your picture say about you? Now check out the before and after profile. Big difference in the impression you get!

I am not expecting you to get a professional picture taken; a good old camera will do the job.

Think, picture = professional. You could argue that this will depend on your profession, so feel free to have a think about what this means for your industry or brand.

Experience

This section is very similar to the work history section of your CV/Resume. Think of it as a CV/Resume and make sure you are not just putting the dates and position of your last roles, add your accomplishments for each role.

What did you achieve for the company? Remember to use hard facts and statistics where possible!

If you can do this, you can show a prospective employer why they should hire you.

Make sure your descriptions are concise and to the point, and remember you are writing this on LinkedIn - so unlike your CV/Resume, you may not have a specific job in mind when writing this.

Another tip for the perfect experience section on LinkedIn is to include instances of certain keywords that will help you to be found by Recruiters and Hiring Managers.

Skills and expertise

You can include skills and expertise in the endorsements section on LinkedIn (see *"Figure 3"*). Recruiters can use LinkedIn's advanced search features to find people by the skills and expertise they feature in their endorsements section.

So in this sense, this is relevant, but let's be frank - anyone can endorse you without knowing very much about you or what you do, so don't worry about this too much!

Figure 3

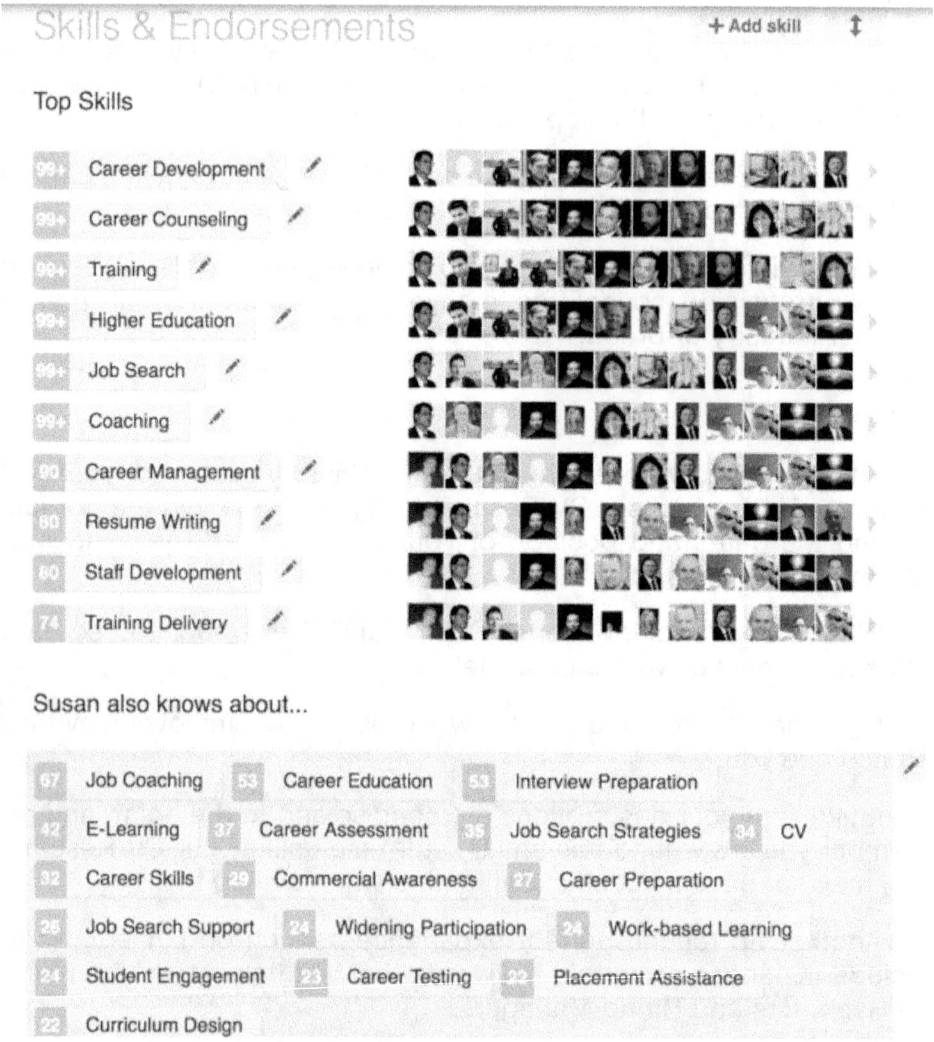

Skills & Endorsements

Top Skills

- 99+ Career Development
- 99+ Career Counseling
- 99+ Training
- 99+ Higher Education
- 99+ Job Search
- 99+ Coaching
- 90 Career Management
- 80 Resume Writing
- 80 Staff Development
- 74 Training Delivery

Susan also knows about...

- 67 Job Coaching
- 53 Career Education
- 53 Interview Preparation
- 42 E-Learning
- 37 Career Assessment
- 35 Job Search Strategies
- 34 CV
- 32 Career Skills
- 29 Commercial Awareness
- 27 Career Preparation
- 26 Job Search Support
- 24 Widening Participation
- 24 Work-based Learning
- 24 Student Engagement
- 23 Career Testing
- 22 Placement Assistance
- 22 Curriculum Design

Add 10-20 of your top skills first. Make sure they are relevant to the type of job you are looking for though.

Recommendations

Recommendations are the bread and butter of a good LinkedIn profile. They are far more valuable than endorsements. If you can harness the power of LinkedIn, they will help you create a very attractive profile.

In any executive or senior role, recommendations will be hugely important in landing that job. Of course, any Hiring Manager or Recruiter is going to be impressed to see how many of your colleagues and past bosses have spoken highly of you. Additionally, the fact that they have taken the time to write something about you on LinkedIn shows that they really truly feel that way.

Obtaining recommendations is not a difficult feat. All you have to do is ask for them! However, you do need to recognise that people are busy. Your request for a recommendation is probably not their top priority, even if you are great friends. It's important to have patience and also to craft a message that will get you that feedback, without you seeming like a nag.

Step one, you must always write a personal request for a recommendation. Please **never** consider using the standard message LinkedIn provides you with, see *Figure 4* below. If you want someone to provide you with a great recommendation – you must personalise it first!

Figure 4

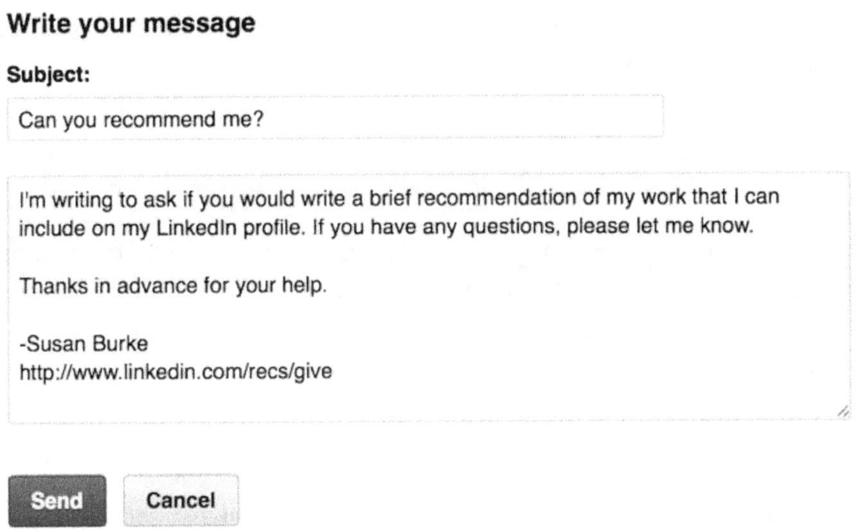

Write your message

Subject:

Can you recommend me?

I'm writing to ask if you would write a brief recommendation of my work that I can include on my LinkedIn profile. If you have any questions, please let me know.

Thanks in advance for your help.

-Susan Burke
http://www.linkedin.com/recs/give

Send   Cancel

I would rather that you said something like the below message. Obviously, feel free to tweak and amend to best suit the individual that you're writing to, but I'm sure you get my drift.

> Hi <Name>
>
> I hope that you're well.
>
> I'm updating my LinkedIn profile and I was wondering whether you would be open to providing me with a recommendation?
>
> If you are open to recommending me in my position as (insert position) but are not sure what to write, I am happy to provide you with some ideas if that would help?
>
> I recognise you are busy, so if I don't hear back from you by late next week, I will follow-up with you again to see if this is possible.
>
> Many thanks
>
> <Your Name>

Why is this message better?

Well, for one we have personalised it. Secondly, you have suggested that you would be happy to provide a couple of ideas, to make it easier for them to write the recommendation. However, the best bit is the fact you have said that you will follow up with this person, so it will be of no surprise to that person when you do. This avoids you appearing pushy and by following up, you have shown yourself to be a person that keeps their word.

So there you have it. By the end of this chapter, you should be well on your way to a revamped CV/Resume and LinkedIn profile. Both working better at attracting Hiring Managers, Recruiters and also being highly visible on Google and Applicant Tracking Software.

Summary

- Make your headline and profile picture stand out.
- Include keywords so you can be found.
- Ask for recommendations, use my template!
- Add your LinkedIn URL to your business card and CV/Resume.

Break Down the Four Walls of the Company You Work In

You're great at your job. You know it and I know it.

I know this when I speak with you.

I can tell how committed you are and what you want and all the great things you've done.

However, it's like you and I are in a secret club, and we are the only ones who know how great you actually are.

The secret club you and I belong to involves you using a crappy CV/Resume and an average LinkedIn profile.

You're modest you see. Well I can only say that you are modest because when I speak to you, I learn so many great things about you, but at times it can be like pulling teeth to get it out of you. However, I get there, I keep pushing and asking and then I find out things that can take you from average to outstanding….

- You're writing a book, and it was closely related to work!

- You've won awards, been put forward for something or praised for something…

- You've restructured your department and in the process achieved great things like I don't know; improved sales, processes - you get what I mean!

Yet all I hear when I see your LinkedIn profile or CV/Resume is some buzz words such as I'm a great team leader, I'm motivated or driven. Well OMG! So are the rest of the population – I thought you were different!

I know you do a great job.

The trouble is, you may well have done a good job BUT, you've also done a really great job of hiding it. And…

- Of blending in and of being mediocre.

- Of being an average Joe Blogs – basically you are VANILLA!

- Of belonging to the secret job club where no-one knows how great you are.

I believe the ideal candidate exists; you've just done a great job of being invisible.

You need to treat yourself as a business, the consequences if you don't, are huge.

Being able to develop you as a business will mean that your message will get outside of the four walls you currently work in. Want to understand exactly what I mean see picture 1 below, you maybe great in your job – but the only people who know this is your employer!

Picture 1

When you learn to do this, you will build yourself as the 'go to person'.

You will get job opportunities coming to you before they are even advertised.

This is how I help my clients, and I would love to help you too, get in touch![21] I do actively practice what I preach, well you're reading this book, aren't you?

Are you ready, or are those four walls going to keep you invisible?

Success isn't a simple road. Sometimes people don't recognise that success is a twisted and long winding journey. It is critical to understand this so that you don't give up just because you have hit a downward spike! *Figure 5* shows you exactly what I mean; this is why I say that sometimes, getting someone to assist you, can help you to avoid all of the ups and downs!

Figure 5

I practice what I preach, and although I've been self-employed for two years now, I received a LinkedIn message from someone I didn't know on LinkedIn, but who had heard of me and wanted to offer me a senior position in relation to Careers in a software company, see *Figure 6, page 46*.

---

21   https://www.linkedin.com/in/susanburkecareers

Figure 6

May 26, 5:47 PM

An opportunity for you?

Dear Susan,

Hello I hope that you are well.

I have been asked to get in contact with you by a client of ours who is looking to fill a number of senior and specialist roles which they would like to bring to your attention.

I would welcome the opportunity to explain further on the phone and wondered when you might be free to talk?

The reason that this happened, is because I have been able to highlight my accomplishments well to both the people I have worked with and networked with, but also to the outside world. This company who wanted to hire me, had not met me, however, they had heard of me!

Build connections

Spend some time every day trying to build your network. Go to after work networking sessions and meet professionals in different industries. Try not to go with work in mind and try not to sell yourself too hard as this can sometimes put people off. Just meet people and build relationships with them so that when there is an opportunity, you are at the forefront of their minds.

When you're not building relationships face-to-face you should be trying to network online. Focus on LinkedIn but that doesn't mean you can't connect with people on Twitter or have a business Facebook page either.

Be accountable

The only person getting in the way of your success is you. It's not like making a New Year's resolution where you spend a few months on it and then have forgotten about it by March. Success and commitment to the goal is a daily battle; it's not something that will suddenly become easy. It always takes effort and focus. You have to commit each day to re-affirm what you want to achieve, otherwise just like a New Year's resolution, it gets forgotten about. This is why the Bootcamp Job Club[22] can really help you succeed!

I can predict that the job search process has caused you some headaches and challenges along the way. In some senses, I see myself as a sort of GP as I've seen/heard it all before, and I say this in a nice way; I'm really just interested in how I can help you to get what you want. So whether that is a move back to be nearer to your family, or to stop you moving away, or maybe it's the next big break, or you're looking for the side move – whatever reason you have for looking for that next executive position, I will do everything I can to help you land it. Why not schedule a call today?[23] (for more details on what this covers, check out *page 27*, the Breakthrough Session to getting you hired).

Summary

- Get noticed for the things you have achieved in your company.
- Schedule some time every day to better yourself.
- Network.
- Be accountable and recognise your own procrastination.

Treat Yourself as a Business

You should have already started to notice that the most important thing in your Job Search Strategy, is the need for you to treat yourself as a business. In the same way that a Hiring Manager needs a candidate with a certain skill set, this is a business transaction after all, you get paid for that skill set at the end of the month.

You can feel the quality of a product through touching it…but you can't quite do this with a service, can you?

---

22 https://linkedinsuccessacademy.com/bootcamp-job-club/

23 https://susanburkecareers.acuityscheduling.com/schedule.php?appointmentType=1160277

So how do you show to the Hiring Managers and Recruiters that you are top quality?

Let's imagine the scenario of booking a hotel. You get a recommendation from a friend about a hotel and visit their website to find out more. However, the quality of their website doesn't match the description of the hotel your friend gave. The website reflects a two-star hotel, compared to the five-star hotel that your friend described.

What I'm trying to say here is that you want to be impressed and intrigued, you want to know more, and you want to get excited that you're going away! That type of excitement is not going to happen with a two-star hotel or a two star LinkedIn profile. Are you going to book that hotel? Probably not! The same goes with the two-star candidate, no matter how good they're supposed to be!

As soon as a Hiring Manager or Recruiter looks at your CV/Resume, they are going to search for you online. The first thing they are likely to find is your LinkedIn profile because it's always highly ranked in search results.

The clues to quality are subtle and are often hiding in your CV/Resume or LinkedIn profile. An incomplete profile, for example, can show someone that you just don't care enough about your future, or you lack attention to detail. Is this a sign of someone who should be hired for an executive position? Probably not!

For your business (Me Ltd.), you need to be a five-star business. You need to ooze five-star quality in everything you do. A selfie on your LinkedIn profile, for example, may give the impression that you haven't put any time and effort into finding an image that suits your target market and audience. Perhaps you could even look flippant. See *"Figure 2"* on *page 37*, to see what I mean.

When a Recruiter or Hiring Manager scans your Resume/CV, they get an impression about you. Ask yourself what impression are you giving off? So whether you are seeking a job or not – you still want to get opportunities coming to you right? Therefore, you need to grasp this approach.

So, be honest with yourself - how are you levelling up? How would you rate yourself? Yes, be honest because this is the only way you are going to be able to improve your profile for the better.

You and I are not much different! If you want to continue to get hired, you do need to treat yourself as a business, and this is about promoting yourself and ultimately learning to get your message out into the real world.

What if, you've already got a job, but you're starting to realise that you need to move on?

Have you ever considered using your existing employer to find your next job? If you're employed now, this is a great tactic to consider…

The great thing about this strategy is that while you are in a role that makes you unhappy, you can still motivate yourself and keep yourself busy. This makes the working day a lot easier and the depression of being in a job you hate subside.

Get training

Work out what training is available, something that is not just useful for your current role, but could also be relevant for your next position.

Go networking

Don't forget to network - don't be blatant about the fact that you are looking for a new job, but make sure that you start connecting with everyone you meet on LinkedIn, and if they could be relevant to you in the future, suggest you meet up for a chat. LinkedIn is a great way to network check out the four FREE video series[24] to learn how and what you can do today!

Be a member of a professional association

Are you a member of a professional association? Well, why not join one and see if your employer is willing to pay your membership, or worst case scenario, contribute to it. Start making yourself known. Find out what you can do to get yourself noticed. Maybe attend a few networking meetings, see if you can get actively involved in events and conferences or maybe contribute as a key note speaker. Look at ways to challenge that comfort zone!

All this is, is a strategy for investing in yourself or getting your current employer to invest in you. If you don't invest in yourself, how are you going to achieve anything new and exciting? Everything you do needs to be better, instead of the same old carbon copy stuff you used to do.

---

24   https://sueburkecareers.leadpages.net/linkedin-free-video-training/

Your USP will be the string that links all of your tools together. That includes your CV/Resume, your LinkedIn profile, your business cards, your social media, your email signature, your website and your interview preparation toolkit[25].

When you bring these all together to communicate to your targeted prospective employer, you have to show your USP, why you should be hired and at the same time relay the same message in a way that presents you to be a five-star quality hire.

Think of it like baking a cake it's a great analogy to use!

Just like baking and almost everything else you will do in your life, you need to have a recipe. We need to work out that shopping list – what's on our list that's going to help you GET that job? The great thing with this type of shopping is that it can add thousands to your bank account – well only if you know what needs to be in that shopping bag!

Your shopping list in order to get that job you would love, is as follows...

- A dollop of resilience.
- A healthy dose of persistence.
- A winning Resume/CV and a robot friendly one as well!
- A well-crafted LinkedIn profile.
- A game plan to focus your efforts.
- The ability to learn how to sell you!
- Interview skills that get you noticed for the RIGHT reasons!
- The ability to network on and offline.
- A fully mapped out job search approach.
- Building you as a brand.
- Creating a two-way job search funnel (oh come on, admit it you're doing it one way, just applying for job after job!)
- Keeping motivated / enjoying the process!

---

25   https://linkedinsuccessacademy.com/interview-toolkit-4/

- Learning that to get HIRED, you need to get NOTICED. Don't panic if you are an introvert; this is not a one size fits all approach.

- Killing procrastination at the root!

Optional

- Getting your employer to help you find your next job.

- Getting insurance if you think you could be made redundant – do read the fine print though to make sure the policy is a valid one!

- Reducing costs - for example, switching temporarily to interest only repayments on your mortgage, etc.

Summary

- The best Job Search Strategy starts when you treat yourself as a business.

- Bring a five-star quality to everything you do.

- Get your employer to invest in you so that you have more skills when you move on.

- Don't forget to also invest in yourself!

- Make sure you get everything on your shopping list so that you have the perfect recipe for success.

The Money is in Your Message

In the last chapter I talked about having a full on toolkit which included your CV/Resume, your LinkedIn profile, your business cards, your social media, your email signature and your website. These all string together with a common theme, your USP.

This is your message. And you need to get your message out to the right audience. In this case, the right employers. Once you start sending your message out, you need to continue in order to avoid being thought of as a one-hit wonder.

Just like an artist who makes it to the charts once and is never seen again, you don't want to be approached by one good company and then realise later that it was, in fact, a fluke!

Since you are treating yourself like a business, you should be paying attention to every detail and continuously thinking about how you will be seen from an outsider's point of view.

One of the most well-known and useful tools to analyse this is social media. With websites such as LinkedIn and Twitter, you can have a steady stream of posts relaying your message, and you can continue to network with others for as long as your professional career remains. However, like anything else, you've got to understand how to use it – because there are REAL dangers. However, these do not outweigh the benefits; I'm only mentioning this to make you aware and not to 'put you off'! There is a difference, and these errors are not just made by kids, but by people at all levels in their careers and of all ages – it's universal!

Sometimes, it can just be an error in judgement sprouting from saying something which you thought was funny but may not be deemed amusing to other people; this can really set you back.

Other times it could simply be a matter of not recognising that you're in a public forum and maybe even getting heated up because of what someone said online. So it leads to a tit for tat or a slanging match. Personally I'm not interested.

Obviously, the more vocal you are online – the more you risk people not agreeing with you. However, if you want to shut people up, the easiest thing is to be nice. When someone says something negative, I will say thanks, wishing you a fantastic day – best wishes Sue. In reality, there is nothing to come back to from this.

What can someone say? Not much and if they do, well don't respond. You can also block people. I am not trying to put you off in terms of becoming more visible, but yes it could happen, so I'm just pre-warning you so that if it does, you know how to handle it.

Here are a few examples[26] of where your message can completely fail to come across on social media and you can lose your job because of it:

---

26   http://mashable.com/2011/06/16/weinergate-social-media-job-loss/#gallery/xx-people-whose-tweets-have-impacted-their-jobs/50bddfb731829767ca0003c9

Connor

In March 2009, Connor was offered a job at Cisco at 22 years old. As any youngster would, she headed to social media to tweet about her job opportunity, see Figure 7.

Figure 7

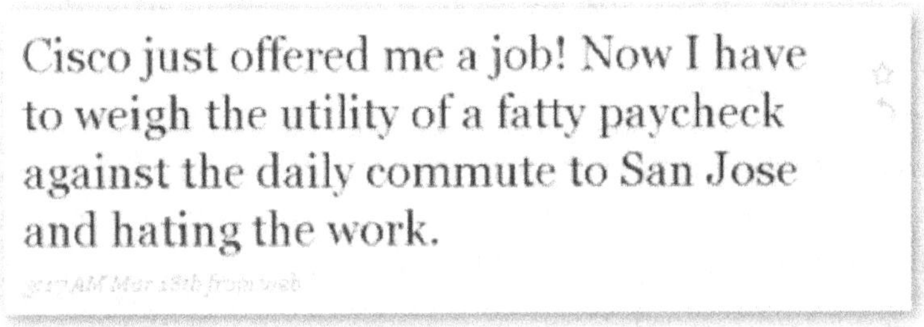

> Cisco just offered me a job! Now I have to weigh the utility of a fatty paycheck against the daily commute to San Jose and hating the work.

A Cisco employee responded to this tweet, offering to pass her sentiments over to her Hiring Manager and she shortly after lost her job, before she had even spent her first day there.

Anthony Weiner

Former member of the United States House of Representatives, Anthony Weiner was fired for sending several explicit photos of himself as a link in a tweet to a 21-year-old girl. The images were meant to be in a private message but sadly Anthony had mixed up his Direct Message (DM) and public message tweet buttons (that tweet button means that his message went out to EVERYONE as opposed to the Direct Message which would have been sent as a private message to the person in question – what a blunder!)

Let's look at how social media can be put to good use

Celia Ampel

Celia Ampel was working as an intern for the Miami Herald. At the time she was using Twitter avidly and was getting ambitious with the people she followed. She followed the Managing Editor of the South Florida Business Journal, who spotted her and liked her profile. They had a job open which involved social media work and offered it to Ampel because she had already proved that she knew what she was doing.

Celia got lucky in that the person she followed was also social media savvy and on the lookout for someone to hire. Many people just aren't that clued up, and they won't be thinking 'I might find an amazing candidate through social media'. So sometimes you have to get bold and ask someone if THEY have an opportunity instead of waiting for an opportunity to come to you.

Want another great story about someone else who got hired via Social Media?

Charlie Loyd[27], a self-described satellite image enthusiast, perfected a better way to make maps with his customized approach to cloudless imagery[28]. He tweeted a sample of his work to five top mapping companies. One of them, @MapBox, replied within three minutes.

That Tweet led to a phone call, an in-person interview, and ultimately, a job offer.

While Charlie's experience happened very quickly, this isn't the first time someone has landed a job because of a Tweet. Job seekers can use Twitter for industry-specific networking chats (see this Tweet Chat Schedule for different industries[29] for a list of times and industries) and as a way to highlight their best work.

It's not just job-seekers who use Twitter. Increasingly, employers use Twitter for real-time recruiting. For instance, National Public Radio uses Twitter to find people who are the right match for the company's needs and ethos.

Thomas Smith, in his book "Successful Advertising" in 1885, makes the following reflections on advertising and messaging:

The 1st time people look at an ad; they don't see it.

The 2nd time, they don't notice it.

The 3rd time, they are aware that it is there.

The 4th time, they have a fleeting sense that they've seen it before.

---

27   https://stories.twitter.com/en/get_a_job.html
28   http://www.flickr.com/photos/vruba/8462449879/
29   http://tweetreports.com/twitter-chat-schedule/

The 5th time, they actually read the ad.

The 6th time, they thumb their nose at it.

The 7th time, they get a little irritated with it.

The 8th time, they think, "Here's that confounded ad again."

The 9th time, they wonder if they're missing out on something.

The 10th time, they ask their friends or neighbours if they've tried it.

The 11th time, they wonder how the company is paying for all these ads.

The 12th time, they start to think that it must be a good product.

The 13th time, they start to feel the product has value.

The 14th time, they start to feel like they've wanted a product like this for a long time.

The 15th time, they start to yearn for it because they can't afford to buy it.

The 16th time, they accept the fact that they will buy it sometime in the future.

The 17th time, they make a commitment to buy the product.

The 18th time, they curse their poverty because they can't buy this terrific product.

The 19th time, they count their money very carefully.

The 20th time prospects see the ad; they buy what it is offering.

So even in 1885, it was observed that advertising is not recognised immediately. You need to dedicate yourself to spreading your message to your audience over a long period of time and to experiment with new, bold ways of getting your message across to your audience.

In advertising, this is called 'effective frequency'. There are different arguments about whether or not three times is the sweet spot, or seven, or even twenty. Who's to know, but remembering something involves repeating it. That is a FACT.

The first goal is to establish a trusted relationship with the person. Maybe enticing them towards you with an article you have written that might help them. Once you have built a relationship, it's easier to start talking about business.

This kind of persistent dedication is what will lead to a positive opportunity like a job.

If you can keep your messaging consistent and show off your USP, then there's no doubt you will be recognised on social media for your hard fought efforts.

Summary

- Don't be a one-hit wonder, continue to send out your message to your audience.

- Your online profile should be just as professional as you are offline at work. Avoid making a social media blunder and costing yourself your own reputation.

- Use effective repetition to get your message out there and have it remembered.

- Build relationships with people first, then once you have developed a relationship you can start talking job opportunities.

A Job Search Strategy is not a CV/Resume Strategy!

Just because you have a CV/Resume doesn't mean you have a Job Search Strategy. Posting your CV/Resume to multiple job opportunities might land you a job but this isn't the way to be consistent and have a redundancy plan. You need to go further than this, take a look at *"Figure 8"*, *page 58-59*, this is a sneak peak of the strategy I use for my VIP clients for the Bootcamp Job Club, you can download your own copy here[30].

The difference with using all of these different mediums is that you are influencing your target audience with repetition and branding. You are treating yourself as a business, and therefore showing your target audience how you can solve their problem and why they should hire you!

---

30   https://app.box.com/s/os5pkfxwiw6w5ieqiu12gk3sc3z95ust

Old Way	New Way
Ad Hoc	Daily
CV/Resume Strategy	Job Search Strategy
Learn by DIY	Strategic
One-way system – you do all the hard work!	Two-way system which attracts companies / people to you
Intrinsic - be great within the 4 walls you work	Professional – build the Like, Know, Trust Factor – (be great outside of those 4 walls!)

In order to truly start your new Job Search Strategy, you need to make the following four changes:

See yourself as a business

Move from being good at your job to translating this outside of the four walls in which you work. You have to treat yourself as a business otherwise you're always going to be stuck in the same situation.

So you want to get hired now? Well if I were to look into a crystal ball, you never know, in the next four years you might want the same thing again (or shock horror the decision is made for you – that is, redundancy could be on the cards).

Wouldn't it be great to learn some skills for life and work out how you get your message outside to Recruiters/Hiring Managers so that you're never stuck for job offers again?

I teach people to get hired, but ultimately, I teach you how to never find yourself in this situation again. This leads on to 'getting you noticed' and how to keep your profile engaging even once you've been hired so that you're always on the market and therefore open to any great, new opportunities that may come directly to you.

Nita is a client of mine and what she realised is she needs to see herself as a business. This was a complete change around in how she previously managed her career. What she was finding was when she had finished the interim role in finance it could lead to months without employment searching for the next position, she realised she was losing out on thousands of

MAP YOUR JOB SEARCH

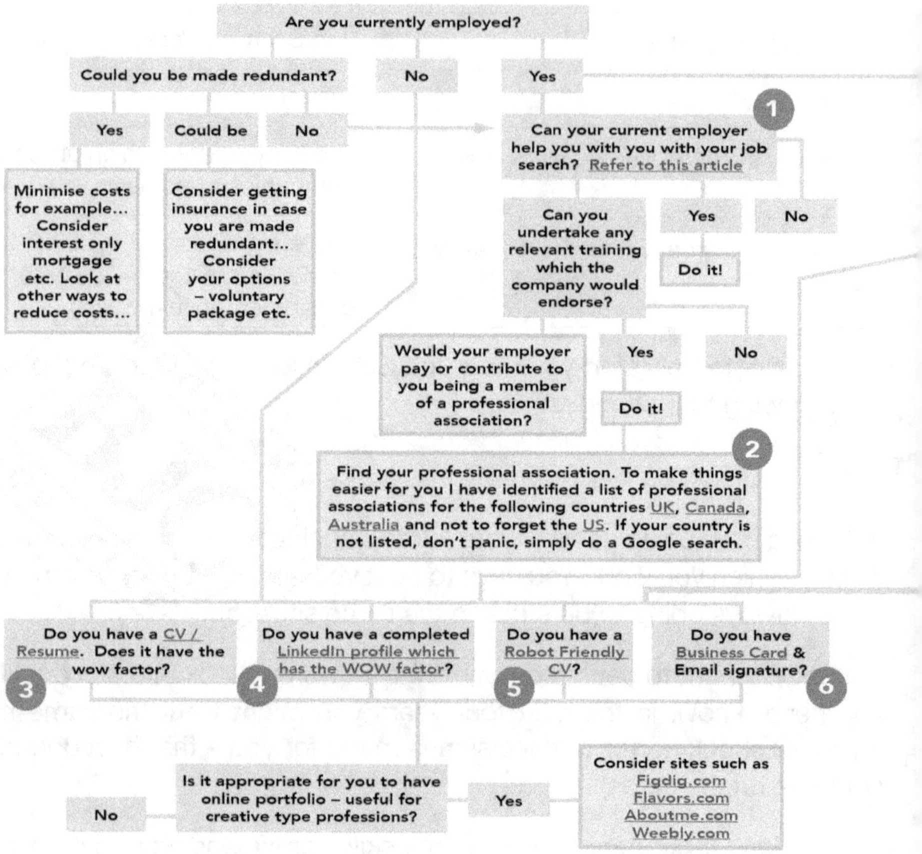

Are you currently employed?

- **Could you be made redundant?** / **No** / **Yes**

Could you be made redundant?
- Yes / Could be / No

Yes: Minimise costs for example... Consider interest only mortgage etc. Look at other ways to reduce costs...

Could be: Consider getting insurance in case you are made redundant... Consider your options – voluntary package etc.

Yes (employed): ① Can your current employer help you with you with your job search? Refer to this article

- Can you undertake any relevant training which the company would endorse? — Yes → Do it! / No
- Would your employer pay or contribute to you being a member of a professional association? — Yes → Do it! / No

② Find your professional association. To make things easier for you I have identified a list of professional associations for the following countries UK, Canada, Australia and not to forget the US. If your country is not listed, don't panic, simply do a Google search.

③ Do you have a CV / Resume. Does it have the wow factor?

④ Do you have a completed LinkedIn profile which has the WOW factor?

⑤ Do you have a Robot Friendly CV?

⑥ Do you have Business Card & Email signature?

Is it appropriate for you to have online portfolio – useful for creative type professions? — No / Yes → Consider sites such as Figdig.com, Flavors.com, Aboutme.com, Weebly.com

ARE YOU READY TO CREATE A THREE WAY FUNNEL OF...

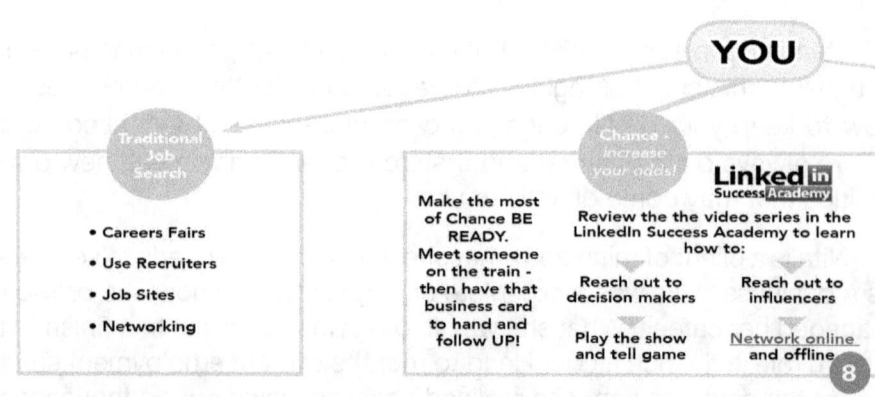

YOU

Traditional Job Search
- Careers Fairs
- Use Recruiters
- Job Sites
- Networking

Chance – increase your odds!
Make the most of Chance BE READY. Meet someone on the train - then have that business card to hand and follow UP!
- Play the show and tell game

LinkedIn Success Academy
Review the the video series in the LinkedIn Success Academy to learn how to:
- Reach out to decision makers
- Reach out to influencers
- Network online and offline ⑧

SUSAN BURKE | 59

Figure 8

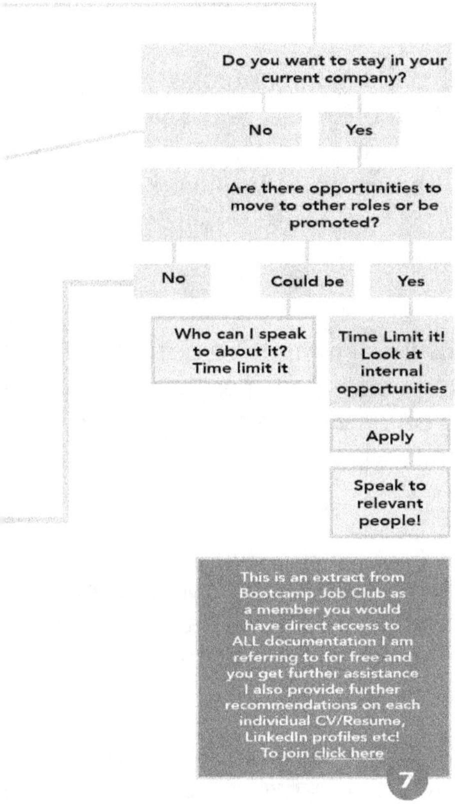

```
                    Do you want to stay in your
                          current company?
                    ┌──────────┬──────────┐
                    No                   Yes
                                          │
                              Are there opportunities to
                              move to other roles or be
                                       promoted?
                    ┌──────────┬──────────┬──────────┐
                    No        Could be            Yes
                    │            │                  │
            Who can I speak    Time Limit it!
            to about it?       Look at
            Time limit it      internal
                               opportunities
                                    │
                                  Apply
                                    │
                               Speak to
                               relevant
                               people!
```

This is an extract from Bootcamp Job Club as a member you would have direct access to ALL documentation I am referring to for free and you get further assistance I also provide further recommendations on each individual CV/Resume, LinkedIn profiles etc! To join click here

1. https://www.linkedin.com/pulse/get-your-employer-help-you-find-next-job-susan-burke

2.
   - UK http://www.totalprofessions.com/profession-finder
   - Canada http://www.cpmdq.com/htm/org.canada2.htm
   - Australia http://www.journoz.com/ausproforgs.html#Accountancy
   - US https://en.wikipedia.org/wiki/Category:Professional_associations_based_in_the_United_States

3. https://www.linkedinsuccessacademy.com/infinite-figure-resume-service/

4. https://www.linkedinsuccessacademy.com/linkedin-rehab-clinic/

5. https://www.linkedinsuccessacademy.com/bumperpackage/

6. https://www.linkedinsuccessacademy.com/bumperpackage/

7. https://www.linkedinsuccessacademy.com/bootcamp-job-club/

8. https://www.linkedinsuccessacademy.com/linkedin-success-academy/

...JOB OPPORTUNITIES (YOU) BEING THE CENTRE OF IT!

Get jobs coming to you... BRAND YOU

- Journals
- Videos
- Writing a book
- Blogs
- Presenting at conferences
- Newspapers/Magazines
- Webinars

pounds of potential earnings. What we realised although she was MORE than capable of doing these roles – the Foundations were just not acting as BAIT to attract companies to her. We changed this, though and within 4 weeks she got the JOB and then the new improved LinkedIn profile was still attracting companies to her, she was, in fact, getting companies chasing her. She has become more visible

So if you are freelancer, contractor or seeking Interim roles you, more so than others, need to recognise YOU are a business, and YOU actively need to be attracting companies to you, even when you get the job, (however this also goes for those on the 9 – 5pm roles as well) you've got to become more visible!

Work smarter not harder!

When I speak to job seekers, 99% of the time they've got a CV/Resume strategy NOT a Job Search Strategy and trust me, there is a big difference. Come on, when you're relying on only one element in your job hunt, your chances of getting hired are pretty damn low!

Develop the bait!

Don't underestimate the basics. The basics are like the foundations of a house. The foundations are key. The foundations are the bait! If you are and I were going fishing, we would need some bait and in the same way, you need bait to lure hirers in.

The bait explains why a company should hire you. If you've not yet managed to figure this out, and this is NOT articulated in your key documents, you dramatically reduce your chances of getting in front of the Hiring Manager. This is how I can help you!

Now, once you've developed your bait, want to see how this then works in practice? You get people interested IN YOU. Remember I said that I practice what I preach, well here it is... For confidentially reasons, I've removed the names of the people who have contacted me, but I wanted to highlight to you that this approach works, and it can work for you too. Imagine having people asking about how YOU can help them day after day. Remember I said to you, yes I am a business but you and I are no different, regardless of whether you are fully employed or self-employed like me? You, like me, need to get people wanting to find out more about you, and yes there is a strategy to this!

Susan Bur

Dear Susan

Thank you for your prompt reply. Also, thank you for endorsing me always seeking to develop / grow. As such, I would greatly value h; conversation with you to update on my... see more

Reply

Messages you've missed

Thanks for endorsing me I will be touch over my goals
It would be useful to see how my approach could be adapted
Jeremy

Reply to Jeremy

Hi Susan, to be honest your profile photo attracted my eye when it popped up in a list of recommendations, but your service intrigued me. I'm currently employed but looking to upgrade. I'd like to... see more

Reply to Michael

Still need more convincing? Well, I've got more and more of these and I regularly receive these messages on most days, from all over the world. Meaning that my message transcends borders, which is great for you if you want to move to another state, another country even. However, you don't need to be doing anything as drastic as move country -this approach still works even if you want to stay where you are now.

Dear Susan, Thank you very much for all! I appreciate to read your posts in LinkedIn. Sincerely

Reply

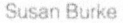 Susan Burke

Thanks Sue. I'm glad to connect as well. I was browsing around and curious about your services. Let's stay connected.
Regards,
Ruth

Reply

 Susan Burke

PHENOMENAL – It is an honor and a privilege to be a part of your network!!
Deepest Gratitude to you for reaching back out to connect.

I am impressed by your summary and your depth of experience!
I... see more

Reply

Find a mentor and invest in yourself

One of the most important things I've done with all of my business, is to find the person who knows more than me on a particular subject, or who is further along with their business, so that I can learn from them.

Sometimes it's a book, a course, a group, or a one on one coaching situation, but those are the most important purchases I've made, to move my business forward.

You need to grab people's attention straight away – get them interested, and get them itching to get in touch because you are the answer to the problem that they have.

Professionals and experts in their field know how to attract the right people, and they know how to entice you to check them out online. I will give you the tools that you need to get people to buy into your brand, to want you on board and to understand your potential value to them.

Filling up space with boring buzz words does not achieve this!

The journey in the pursuit of the best career you can have never ends, and because the journey is complicated and contains many roads, sometimes we are guilty of going the wrong way until we realise that we are completely lost.

However, what happens when all of your hard work suddenly pays off and you have finally got that interview? Well, we need to improve your chances of getting the job!

How to be successful in your job interview

Being seen as extremely professional at interview is easier than you think. I'm about to show you how you can stand head and shoulders above anyone else, just by making sure you follow a couple of rules.

So, for example, if they are hiring a sales manager or business development manager and their end goal is that they want somebody who can sell their business and their products or services, what exactly do they want you to sell and how are they expecting you to do it?

Are they launching a new product? How can you assist? Remember anything that you say must be evidenced with examples of experiences that you have had and what you have done in the past.

Tell them stories of how you have managed to showcase your skills and how you have put them to good practical use in a business environment. What results have you achieved and how did you go about getting there? Don't assume that they have thoroughly read your application, and even if they have, they may well have forgotten as they read so many. Treat the interview as if they know nothing about you. Zero. That way you can't go wrong. Quantify things whenever possible.

In preparation for your interview, check yourself out for any strange mannerisms! If necessary, practice talking to yourself in front of a mirror - I know it sounds a bit mad!

Personally I have a habit of waving my hands around. Not the best look! Work out what your little quirks are and get them in check. I have to lock my hands tight to stop those hands waving around like a mad woman. So what's your thing that you do when the pressure is on, and how are you going to stop yourself doing it?

The next stage is 'BE REMEMBERED'. Regardless of how well you've done. No matter how well you have developed a rapport with the interviewer, remember they are often interviewing many people for the same job in a single day. Make it easy for them to remember you, by using the Employer Toolkit/Interview Toolkit[31], you will be able to fast track your interview success. Checkout the '30 Day Plan' (*"Figure 10"*) and 'What can I offer your company from day one'. See *"Figure 9"*.

The Interview Success Kit is the document showing you how you can decide what you have to offer a company from day one. It's a great document which can be used at interview, if you are after a high level role.

I've never been to an interview where they have not asked the following question at the end of the interview process, "Do you have any questions". You could say, "It's not a question as such, however, I feel strongly that I am the RIGHT candidate and I've prepared this document to show why I feel I am the perfect fit".

This document will also direct people to check you out online – it points them towards your LinkedIn profile. The idea is to leave the document with them, so when they make their decision on who to hire, they remember you. Can you see how it all starts to link together in everything we do? The email signature, the LinkedIn profile, even the documents are all working together not just by themselves!

The 30 Day Plan is great if you have a follow-up interview or if you feel you know enough about the company, bring it with you.

Clients I have worked with have had great success with these docu-

---

31   https://linkedinsuccessacademy.com/interviewsuccesskit/

ments, as Graham actually said when he gained his role:

> "At the end of the first interview, I gave the interviewee my "What I can offer from Day One" document ("Figure 9"). This is another template created by Sue, which is so simple, but is also a work of genius. Nobody else being interviewed will have done anything similar. The second interview went really well and this time I gave the interviewers my "30 Day Plan" document. ("Figure 10"), yes, another of Sue's templates. The feedback that I received from the interviewer was that I was very well prepared, and I went through to the third and final interview. Using all that I had learned, I got through the final interview and was successful in securing the role as the Senior Finance Manager for ▇▇▇ at ▇▇▇▇▇▇".

Figure 9

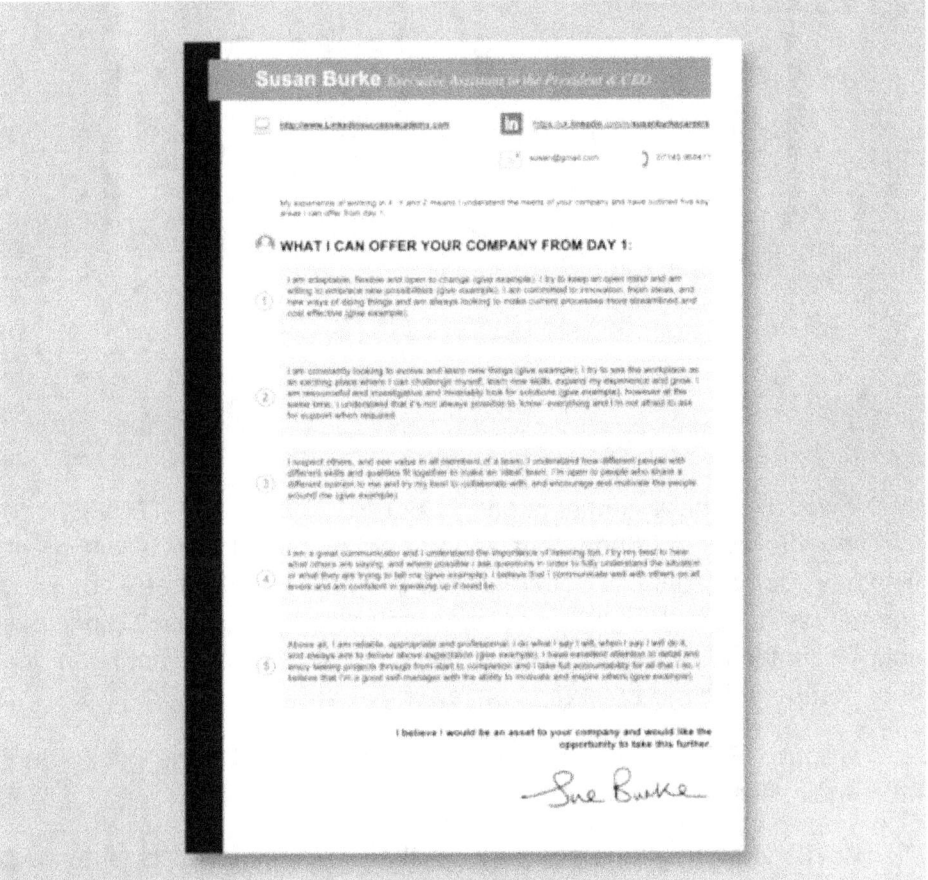

Figure 10

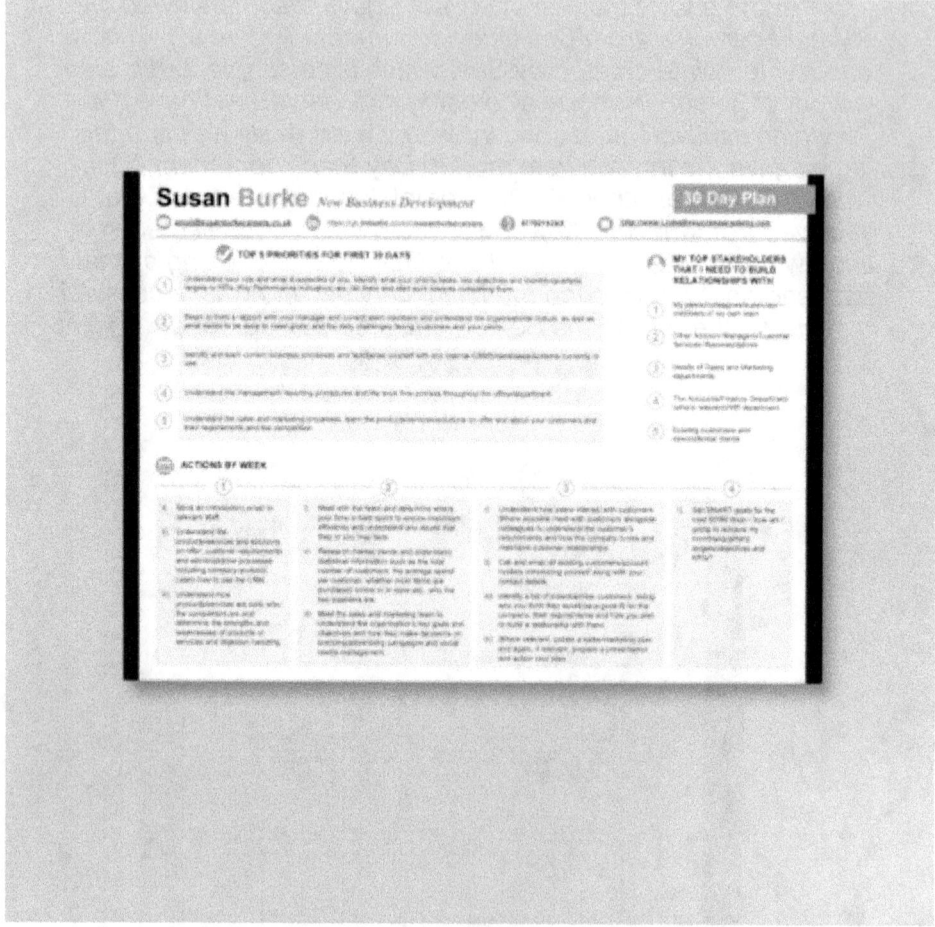

However, these documents can ALSO GET YOU AN INTERVIEW before the interview – I know that sounds crazy, but I know a few clients who have uploaded these documents to Company's Job Sites – you know sometimes it says, "would you like to upload anything else" other than your Resume/CV or applications? Well you could try the "what I can offer your company from day one" as a starter!

I want to REALLY drill this home. So let's consider the background stuff again, this is so important.

- Interviewing you is possibly not their full-time job, this is an additional responsibility.

- Like anyone else, they may have family/friend/personal matters floating around in their head.
- Not to mention the 100 odd emails that will land in their inbox just whilst they are taking time out to interview you.
- They are likely to be interviewing maybe 6 to 8 people in that day.
- They are unlikely to be making a final decision on that day.

This is a REAL problem.

No matter how much rapport you develop at the time of the interview, the fact is, these people are busy, meaning the biggest barrier you face is that they could forget you. If they forget who you are, you don't stand a chance of getting that job, you prepped and prepared for. I don't want this for you.

Summary

- You need to start doing things differently.
- Start by treating yourself as a business, invest in yourself.
- Work smarter not harder, have a strategy.
- Develop the bait, what's going to make you stand out?
- Find a mentor who is wiser than you to give you advice.
- Be remembered when you get that interview.

You're Hired - Don't Stop Now!

Once people secure that all important job, they breathe a sigh of relief, and I want you to feel the same way, but I also want you to go one step further. But first…

Celebrate what you have achieved so far, how many of us actually stop to see how far we have come? This is so important because if you can't see the road you have travelled, you're never going to be happy with what you have achieved so far, there will always be another hurdle to cross. So don't go searching for another task, stop, celebrate and recognise that you've made it.

Reward yourself for what you have achieved. In some sense, I bet it has been like cycling up a mountain, but now you want to change gears because you don't need to go so fast. The steepness of that hill has levelled off slightly, and things should be getting easier. However, YES, after you have recognised what you have achieved you need to select another gear.

So what does second gear look like?

Well, second gear keeps the momentum you have built up in order to find this job and ensures that you will always be working towards that next level.

You want a pay rise or a promotion? Why not?

You want to avoid redundancy? It can happen!

You want companies chasing you?

Just keep your foot on the pedal and keep pushing yourself. Don't fall back into the old school ways as soon as you have found a job. If you like the sound of this you will want to check out my VIP programme – "Get Companies Chasing YOU[32]"

Remember the whole point of this book is to get companies chasing you – this is an ongoing process, it does not stop when you get hired, it just means you shift gear that's all.

I know well and good that it's a problem when you first get a new job as you are so busy with being inducted, meeting new people as well as keeping in touch with your family and friends. It's understandable that the first 3-6 months will take some getting used to, but the great intentions you had to build yourself as the go-to person, just fade away unless you keep up the momentum you have built.

You need to focus now on the branding phase, and you need to do this off your own back, rather than just doing it because I have told you to. If you are reading this book, it's probably because you are motivated enough to find a job. Well, it's time to motivate yourself to continue to brand and position yourself after you get hired. This is the key! Otherwise, you have simply played a game of snakes and ladders (see "*Figure 11*", page 69, and you will end up back at SQUARE 1. Yes, you'll end up back at Chapter 1, tweaking your Resume/CV trying to get people to notice you. You'll have to climb that mountain again – rather than now just being able to treat it as a slow ramp – see the difference. Don't mess with your future, don't under-estimate the importance of your message – otherwise at some point the salary could actually start to decrease, not increase!

---

32   https://www.linkedinsuccessacademy.com/getcompanieschasingyou/

Figure 11

Have you ever noticed how much time people are prepared to invest in searching out their perfect holiday? However, your holiday only lasts for 2 weeks! Your career will last for 50 years or more, yet people often don't recognise that you need to actively invest in Career Management. It is madness really that people will invest so much of their time and energy into a family holiday and yet totally neglect their career. This isn't a two-week holiday; this is the rest of your life and if you don't want to be left behind – you need to invest in YOU.

You can give every excuse in the book, and some of those excuses could be perfectly valid, but sometimes you just have to push through. I am writing this book from my bed, three days after a knee operation, and it would have been a perfectly reasonable excuse not to write this book in my current circumstance, but I didn't allow it to be.

This book is important to me, so I made the time for it and made it my priority.

I'm good at helping you to get the results you want, and it's much faster than having to learn by yourself through trial and error. I'm good at providing accountability because with anything you need to learn; it's all about the discipline. Finally, I'm good at showing you what you can do outside of the barriers you have put up for yourself.

I am human too, and I recognised a long time ago that I couldn't do everything. However, I am a master of getting things done in the quickest time possible. If you would like to know more, I would love to share. Feel free to get in touch, but do also check out the Bootcamp Job Club[33], this is my VIP service after all.

Job Search Re-Invention Toolkit –

Throughout this book I have provided you with great tools to help re-invent your job search. I would love to personally invite you to my LinkedIn Group[34], where you will receive hints and tips not just to gain employment but also to manage your career, starting today. To join my LinkedIn group click here[35].

1. Creative CV/Resume Template – great to upload to your LinkedIn profile or send direct to the hiring manager, click here[36].

---

33   https://linkedinsuccessacademy.com/bootcamp-job-club/
34   https://www.linkedin.com/groups/8291485
35   https://www.linkedinsuccessacademy.com/free-creative-cv-template
36   https://www.linkedinsuccessacademy.com/free-creative-cv-template

2. Get your LinkedIn profile working 24/7 watch the Video Series, click here[37].

This will help you to re-invent your job search, today.

Final Word

Time and time again I see people waiting for others to dictate their future, but this whole book has been about showing you how to take control of your own destiny.

I have been there too, but by taking my own advice I have managed to achieve a great many things such as;

- Being interviewed and published in the Guardian and Telegraph, just by seeking out and building rapport with a journalist in the National Press.
- Getting speaking slots like the National Careers Show in London and Leeds, just by putting myself forward and doing my research to seek out the opportunity.
- Using my salary to re-invest in myself and build my website.
- Using my past employers to upgrade my skill set and get more training or by paying for my own training. Believe me, it was worth every penny.
- Having an online profile that allowed me to get nominated - UK Career Development Institute on their council.

I was in charge of my own personal development, no one else. I learnt that sometimes you have to break the rules and stand outside of the box in order to be noticed. Out of this comes more job opportunities.

So remember this simple recipe for the perfect Job Search Strategy and it starts with pinpointing your USP.

The cost of being unhappy in a job or unemployed can be huge, but you are in charge of your own destiny, and only YOU can make the change you need.

---

37   https://sueburkecareers.leadpages.co/linkedin-free-video-training/

It's about stepping outside of your comfort zone and recognising that using the same old vanilla tactics is over. To stand out, you need to do something different.

Your first step is to rebuild your foundations. Start with that CV/Resume.

- Get rid of all those crappy adjectives!
- Use facts to back up your skills and experience.
- Highlight the impressive stuff.
- Use good design.
- Build a CV/Resume for a Hiring Manager & have another CV ideal for job sites.
- Link to your LinkedIn profile and website.

Now rebuild your LinkedIn profile.

- Create an awesome eye-catching headline.
- Think about what a professional looking photo means for you.
- Remember you want to be found!
- Focus on building quality recommendations.

Everything that you poured into your CV/Resume and LinkedIn profile should ooze your USP. It should shout to the rooftops the kind of BRAND or person you are and most importantly, it should tell Recruiters and Hiring Managers why they should hire YOU.

You might think that you do not have time to do all of this, and if you don't, well, use me!

Part of the formula to success is not procrastinating. You are wasting your evenings in front of the TV. Be true to yourself. If you're really serious about this, you can find the time to spend on it. We should all dedicate at least 20 – 30 mins a day to our self-improvement.

So what should you do with that time?

Spend it researching new things. Apply for an award or a speaking position. Read a report in your industry. Find new companies you want to target.

In many ways, this is much like running your own business. You are in it 24-7 trying to improve it. Building your own business isn't easy, it involves dedication and time. A good business can't expect customers to come running through the door. You have to go out and get those customers and how do you do that?

The first thing is to invest in yourself. Like any business, you should always be trying to improve. Whether this is by paying for tickets to a seminar or conference, signing up for a course or hiring a coach like me – success won't come unless you reach out to the world around you and admit that you don't know it all. There is always something out there you can learn or be better at. Especially since we live in such a fast-paced environment, one minute you know something and the next, all that information is redundant. Keeping up-to-date with new trends and technologies is vital to staying on top of your industry.

If you are working, then maybe a course is not the way to go but have you thought about getting your current employer to invest in you? They don't know you're leaving after all. Of course, you need to stick to something relevant to your current job role, but it's always worth an ask.

It's good to think ahead, and if you are stuck in a job that is making you sick, a training programme or course could be the self-investment you need to get you excited about things again.

Let's go back to your USP again for a minute. You have now had some time to invest in your foundations and start looking into the future. This whole time, you will have been keeping your USP in mind (I hope). This is the string that holds all of your channels together, by channels I mean everything that you are using to create your BRAND - your LinkedIn profile, your social media, your business cards, your email signature, etc.

What you are doing is self-investing in order to continuously improve the quality of the message you are sending out about yourself, and the quality of the people who receive that message.

Being noticed by the right people isn't a secret, a wizard didn't conjure it up in his cauldron. All it takes is putting yourself out in front of the right people and doing it enough times to be remembered. Repetition is key.

Remember we talked about effective repetition? Well, you can send your message out a hundred different ways through a hundred different channels and eventually someone is going to have heard you enough to really take notice. The better the quality brand and message you have, the better you will be at being noticed.

When you have finally reached the last sprint and got the job interview, everything remains the same. Your stories about your successes and your accomplishments will be based on facts, your BRAND will shine through, and your WHY will get you hired. The formula is never complete without that most important piece – you. So let your personality shine through.

If you want to really fast track your success, you should hire a mentor with an understanding of what you should do in order to avoid failure and get hired. I have had many mentors myself in the past years and they have all helped me to shape my personal brand, just as they will you.

So you think you have it all figured out by now huh? Think again! All you've done is read this book so you might have a much better understanding of what you NEED to do, but you still haven't done it yet and, once you get the job you will need to keep doing it.

This isn't just a formula to get you hired. This is a formula that will revamp your career and your authority in your given field.

But wait!

How you and I can work together

1. Want to see the value I can offer, in a low cost, risk-free way, then I promise you - you will love my Career Unplugged Society Membership Programme[38]

Joining the CareerUnplugged.com entitles you to essential resources and benefits that will spin what you thought you knew about

- Job search
- Getting companies chasing you – even when you're hired
- How to manage your career

Accountability – You are NOT alone! You will receive valuable resources every 2 weeks, Q&A every month and membership of our private LinkedIn group where you will meet people who understand the frustrations you are facing.

---

38   https://careerunplugged.com

Ready Written Scripts - You won't have to spend hours writing and re-writing cover letters. Cover letters are so last season! Meet the ground-breaking 'Show and tell' letter! Ensure you get that interview!

Shine at Interview with the Ultimate Interview Success Kit - create a winning impression at interview with the Ultimate Interview Success Kit - Get the exact blueprint of what you should say!

LinkedIn Success Academy - You will become a full member of our celebrated LinkedIn Success Academy. Oh, and did I mention this includes a 20 minute 1-2-1 session with me!

Nail that CV/Resume - Having a slick, superior CV/Resume that stands out from the crowd can ensure you get a face to face interview, you will get Step-by-Step instructions on how to create a 'wow-factor' CV/Resume that clearly shows your Unique Selling Points and why a company should hire YOU!

Building you as a brand - Don't stop just because you've landed that dream job! Learn how to keep companies continually interested in you through your own personal branding. Establish yourself as a thought leader, allowing you to pursue your passion. Open doors, create unique opportunities and push yourself in exciting new directions.

2. Prefer some individual VIP attention – book yourself in for a chat to see the high level services I offer, but please note that I do get many requests per week, if this not possible, I will signpost you to get the support you need, so this is a 100% win/win situation. I've made things even easier for you and done most of the legwork myself. With my Bootcamp Job Club you will have the toolkit for success. I will help you build this entire formula and turn it into something that will not only get you hired, but also get a raise and build a successful career. You can book in for the Breakthrough Job Search session by clicking here[39].

3. Got hired and now want to continue managing your career not giving ownership away? Then it's time to learn the ropes, this is great for job searchers as well. Join my VIP Day, Learn "How to get companies chasing YOU!"[40]

---

39   https://susanburkecareers.acuityscheduling.com/schedule.php?appointment-Type=1160277

40   https://www.linkedinsuccessacademy.com/getcompanieschasingyou/

What will I gain?

1. The first phase - Bait Creation

I will show you what a great profile looks like. I can guarantee that whatever you think is a good profile actually isn't, and this stage is all about stepping your game up. If you want to be noticed, then you have to make yourself worth noticing.

At the end of stage 1, you will have learnt

- How to create your USP – you only get hired based on your USP. The company chooses you because you solve a problem that they have.
- What great LinkedIn profile looks like – many examples, one after the other, from across many industry sectors.
- Why your profile was not grabbing the attention of the recruiter – the faults and flaws listed to you so that you don't make them again!
- What a great CV/resume looks like.
- Why your CV is failing and how you can turn it around so that people actually get in touch after reading it. Your CV/resume is designed to do two things – get you hired and get you interviewed. If you're getting neither – bin it and start again!
- How NOT to do a CV – get ready for some CV shames!
- Why the best CVs are getting people noticed, with examples covering various sectors

2. Second Phase - Audience Identification

We have the foundations, it's time to build up! Let's discover your audience!

- Who are your gatekeepers, and who can help you to climb to the next level?
- Who are the people/companies that could hire you?

We develop a HIT list so that you become visible in your niche – what's the point in getting your message out there if people who aren't relevant to you are the only ones seeing it?

At the end of this stage

- You will feel confident in terms of how to find your gatekeepers/ hiring managers/ no matter where you live in the world you live or what profession you want to work in!
- I will show you step by step...

3. Third Phase - Time to get YOU noticed

I'll show you what I do. I get myself noticed and breakdown the barriers, but I'm not slave and I don't believe that you have to do everything. I know that you are busy, because so am I. I will show you to get the most value without breaking the bank or wasting time.

People will be wondering how you've done it!

It's not a big secret, really – you'll just become more savvy. I will make things easy, digestible and step by step so that you can balance work and social perfectly.

This is a real deal breaker – we all want that balance.

At the end of this stage you will:

- You will feel more confident in getting your message out to the world. We will have created your 'fame plan', like, know & trust factor plan to make this happen.
- We will have worked out what's been holding you back, and have made a plan to stop it!
- Know how to get yourself noticed in a short amount of time.

Do not feel held back because of your industry or country – you will know what to do, and how to do it.

"If it is important you will find a way. If not you'll find an excuse"

As always Get Noticed, Get Hired,

Sue

www.ingramcontent.com/pod-product-compliance
Lightning Source LLC
Chambersburg PA
CBHW070330190526
45169CB00005B/1825